the Dark Side *of* AUTISM

the Dark Side *of* AUTISM

Struggling to Find Peace and Understanding When Life's Not Full of Rainbows, Unicorns and Blessings

Angela Berg-Dallara

NEW YORK

the Dark Side *of* AUTISM
Struggling to Find Peace and Understanding When Life's Not Full of Rainbows, Unicorns and Blessings

© 2014 **Angela Berg-Dallara**.

Published in New York, New York, by Morgan James Publishing. Morgan James and The Entrepreneurial Publisher are trademarks of Morgan James, LLC. www.MorganJamesPublishing.com

The Morgan James Speakers Group can bring authors to your live event. For more information or to book an event visit The Morgan James Speakers Group at www.TheMorganJamesSpeakersGroup.com.

A FREE eBook edition is available with the purchase of this print book

CLEARLY PRINT YOUR NAME IN THE BOX ABOVE

Instructions to claim your free eBook edition:
1. Download the BitLit app for Android or iOS
2. Write your name in UPPER CASE in the box
3. Use the BitLit app to submit a photo
4. Download your eBook to any device

ISBN 978-1-63047-080-7 paperback
ISBN 978-1-63047-081-4 eBook
ISBN 978-1-63047-082-1 hardcover
Library of Congress Control Number:
2013957728

Cover Design by:
Rachel Lopez
www.r2cdesign.com

Interior Design by:
Bonnie Bushman
bonnie@caboodlegraphics.com

In an effort to support local communities, raise awareness and funds, Morgan James Publishing donates a percentage of all book sales for the life of each book to Habitat for Humanity Peninsula and Greater Williamsburg.

Get involved today, visit
www.MorganJamesBuilds.com

Habitat
for Humanity
Peninsula and
Greater Williamsburg
Building Partner

With Love,

For my boys, Jimmy and Dominic

Broken Dreams Poem

As children bring their broken toys
with tears for us to mend,
I brought my broken dreams to God
because He was my friend.
But then instead of leaving Him
in peace to work alone,
I hung around and tried to help
with ways that were my own.
At last I snatched them back and cried,
"How could you be so slow"
"My child," He said, "What could I do?
You never did let go."

—*written by Robert J. Burdette*

TABLE OF CONTENTS

ONE

INTRODUCTION

"More children will be diagnosed with autism this year
than with AIDS, diabetes, and cancer combined."
—**Bob Wright**, Cofounder, Autism Speaks

MY REALITY

'm a 46-year-old mother of a nonverbal little boy with autism and
epilepsy. This is the story of how Dominic, my husband, my older
son, and I are navigating through a brand new world – and not
always in a positive world of special needs.

It's been six years. Six years of HELL since we found out. There I
said it. HELL, and I capitalized it. Six years of wondering and guessing
and grieving and still not knowing what exactly is wrong with my son
and why. Six years of worrying about a completely unpredictable future

for him and for my family and me. Six exhausting years of pretending to be okay, with a simulated smile plastered on my face, while trying to maintain an image of a super mom. Six years of being Dominic's voice since he has none and rooting him on, so that he, my family, and I can find our place in this new and very different and mostly scary world.

Not many parents are telling the truth about what it's like to have a child with severe autism or epilepsy. The word "special" is politically correct, but it's a misnomer. A more misleading word couldn't have been chosen. "Special" is deceptive since it connotes something great. Why would you want to refer to so many debilitating challenges that people face as *special*?

Special implies something positive, but autism, epilepsy, blindness, deafness, cerebral palsy, muscular dystrophy, mental retardation, Down Syndrome and all the other "special needs" complexes and diseases are something mostly difficult and frustrating. If you only remember one thing after reading this book, may it be –

"There's nothing special about special needs."

It doesn't help or comfort me to know that one in every 54 boys will be diagnosed with ASD (Autism Spectrum Disorder). At the time of his diagnosis Dominic was just 14 months old. I was told by his couldn't-be-any-less-helpful pediatrician that I was overreacting. I was made to feel crazy and small and even doubt my maternal instincts, even though I knew something wasn't right with his development. After insisting on a second opinion, it was determined that he was indeed on the autism spectrum, whatever that meant.

Once your child is diagnosed, the autism spectrum is so long and vast you just never know where he or she may end up. My son was given a generic and vague label, PDD/NOS which stands for Pervasive Development Disorder/Not Otherwise Specified. I don't think they could have come up with a more vague description of what was going on with my son's brain. To say I was more confused when I left that appointment would be an understatement!

Like so many, I turned to books and the internet to find out more about the incredibly challenging life we had in store for us. I poured my heart and soul into researching what I thought was happening. Unfortunately, I found most books weren't talking about the struggles of raising a child with special needs. They were focused on the goodness, the blessing, and the gifts. Sure they might touch on the struggles, but not one was painting the real picture of how much the whole thing sucked. Everything I was reading was happy-go-lucky to the point of ad nauseam. How could I say, "Awe shucks, I got a kiddo with autism, I think I'll sing a Louis Armstrong song and spread the love around."

No matter how hard I tried, I didn't feel that way. I'd end up throwing books at the wall somewhere between Chapters 2 and 5. I was frustrated because I desperately wanted to feel a connection to the parents who were writing these books. I felt guilty and shameful for not feeling the same way they did. I was left scratching my head wondering how these parents were making lemonade out of lemons, and why I could not see the good in what was happening (to us). All I wanted was a lemon martini and to make this nightmare all go away.

I am still looking for advice and a sense of community with other parents who are going through what I am, but it's impossible when no one is telling the truth. I'm writing this book to spread the truth. The reality is most every parent who gets their kid ready for special ed school and to catch a short bus at 7:30 a.m. is exhausted from sleep deprivation the night before. That's a cold hard fact!

It's not all rainbows, roses, and sunshine when you watch your child suffer through a grand mal seizure at age two. It's not magical. I can tell you for sure that it is not a blessing that my seven year old is so doped up on anti-seizure medication that he can't comprehend half of what is going on. It's not a gift that I've never heard my son speak a single word and that he feels he needs to scream and tantrum in order to communicate with us.

I truly believe that blessings come in all shapes and sizes, but raising a completely nonverbal child with severe neuro-challenges is not my idea of being blessed. I don't feel blessed and I'm pretty sure he doesn't feel blessed either. So, please, enough with the BLESSING talk. The only blessing is that he doesn't have anything else to compare his life to since he's been sick and fighting challenges his entire existence. Dominic knows nothing else, but I do. I know all the things that could have been and should have been for him. I know how hard life is going to be for him, he does not.

This book is about the truth of raising a child with special needs, no holds barred and no smoke and mirrors. My words are not meant to hurt, offend, or judge anyone. The most important thing you should understand is this— I can love my son with all the love my heart can hold and still hate what is happening to him and to us as a family.

Special needs parents live in a hush-hush world of secret members who are forced to deal with things that don't get talked about outside of our exclusive club. The underbelly is certainly not disseminated to the mainstream. Because I am speaking out against the majority and telling it like it is, I'm sure there will be judgment that I am belittling those with ASD. This book is not what I think about "them," it's a book about what I think about "it."

Please consider for a moment how people feel about cancer, diabetes, lupus, MS, heart disease, Alzheimer's or dementia when it takes someone that they love. I feel that way about autism.

After hours of therapy and self reflection, I know that it doesn't make me a bad parent or person to have not made peace with the disease, debilitation, disability, impairment, whatever you want to call it, that has paralyzed my son's brain rendering him a thirteen month old in a seven-year-old's body. How can I ever make peace with the fact that my son will never lead an independent life outside of this home or that I may be changing diapers for a very, very long time (possibly forever). While I accept my son's condition, I will never be okay with the fact that he may never speak a single word, tell me that he loves me, or be able to make the simplest request verbally. There's a broad difference between making peace with something and accepting something. I'm not in denial or delusional about my situation. I have come to terms with what Dominic's autism means for us as a family, for me individually, and especially for Dominic.

I chose to be a parent and roll the dice. I don't blame anyone or anything for what's happened, and I do not sit here with a victim mentality. It was a decision that my husband and I made to have children, and with that there was always a risk. I knew about the risk before having both of my kids, which is why I waited so long to have them. Ironically that could be a factor in Dominic's autism. Nothing is guaranteed in life, especially when our health or the health of someone we love is concerned. We are faced with loss and death throughout our lives over and over and over again.

Having a child with special needs, however, is a loss. Thankfully your child is alive but you experience grief for what is happening to everyone involved. I still grieve the loss of having a productive, independent little boy who I had imagined would have a much different life. I grieve the hopes and dreams I had for my son. Now my focus is just getting through the day without incident. We live in survival mode every day.

Thinking of the future is no longer an option for me because it is so very unknown. That's hard for a control freak like me to stomach. A thought that often wakes me in a cold sweat at night is wondering who will care for and love Dominic if something happens to my husband or me. Friends and family members aren't exactly beating down our door to help with Dominic. And do I blame them? No! But a blaring reality is that when I can no longer care for my son, he will most likely end up in some kind of group home, institution or worse.

Optimism has never been my strong suit. And while I'd like to think of myself as a realist, it's probably more fitting to call me a pessimist. My glass has usually been half empty. And, unfortunately my son's glass is really empty right now.

The purpose of this book isn't to unleash and vent as much as it is to touch the hearts of those parents who are also struggling every single day with their special needs child, the way I struggle. It would have saved me thousands of dollars in therapy if there would have been a book available to me that gave me permission to feel sad, lonely, angry, depressed, and feel like I belonged. I longed for a book that didn't alienate me and my darkness. It would have helped me to know that the feelings I was having were somewhat natural and that other parents in my situation might also having them instead of feeling shame for my feelings of despair.

No one seems to be talking about the dark side of autism. I say dark side because besides the sometimes dark, confusing, and complicated side of having autism, there is the dark and perplexing side of caring for someone with autism. The darkness can mean depression, anxiety, lack of sleep, behavioral, health, and developmental issues, anger management, medications, self-control, and I'm still just talking about the caregiver.

When you have strong feelings about something so significant in your life, and you look around to try to find a commonality amongst others who are in a similar situation and you can't, it can make you feel worse. Besides feeling incredibly anxious and worried about your child, you begin second guessing your negative feelings, thinking that there might be something wrong with you. When you're already in a fragile state, the loneliness can be debilitating. Why does the light at the end of the tunnel look more like an oncoming train or short bus? Why can I not see the blessings and the gifts? Why do I not feel "chosen" by God or Buddha or Allah or the baby Jesus? What is wrong with ME?

Some days I cry. Some days I am devastated. Most days I am overtired and depressed. I sigh a lot. My days are defined by the number of seizures, Dominic's health, and whether or not he has hurt himself. If we can get through the day and go to bed without a visit to the hospital or doctor, it's a good day!

You'd think by now I would have answers, tools, and a handle on what is going on and be more equipped to function, but I am a parent heaved headfirst into the (mostly) unknown world of autism. My family's lives were turned upside down. Our world spun out of control faster than you can say *stimming*. (If you don't know what this means, you'll find out soon.)

TWO

AUTISM SPECTRUM DISORDER AND BEYOND

WHAT IS ASD (AUTISM SPECTRUM DISORDERS)?

C hances are, you know someone with autism on the spectrum, but what do you really know about it? Most people think they are familiar with autism simply because they saw the movie, *Rainman*, with Dustin Hoffman and Tom Cruise. While I loved that movie, it is not an accurate representation of most autistic people. It's a very small autistic percentage who are card-counting mathematical genius savants!

The most significant thing about what I have learned about the autism spectrum is this— it is wide and extremely individual. You never really know where someone with an early diagnosis will end up after all is said and done. I have a seven year old on the spectrum and I still don't know. Besides being a moving target, autism is an ironic metaphor for having a predictable amount of unpredictability.

According to www.autismstatistics.com, autism is one of the rare conditions classified under a group of disorders referred to as Autism Spectrum Disorders (ASD). The severity of ASD varies. Some forms of autism are more debilitating while others, like Asperger's, are milder. Children who are affected exhibit a range of deficiencies in learning, social interaction, and communication. It is not known what causes autism, but current studies indicate that genetic and environmental factors play a role.

A survey report released by the Center for Disease Control (CDC) in March 2012 shows that the occurrence of autism in the US is 1 in 88 children. Boys are four times more likely to develop autism than girls.

It is estimated that more than $137 billion is spent on autism in the US each year. This figure is expected to rise in the coming decade. The government appropriates 5% or $269 million of these funds towards research in autism and other less common childhood disorders.

Are we living in a pandemic of autism? The numbers are staggering, but in my opinion, I would say, no we are not. According to many research studies, sources, and professionals, there is no autism epidemic. More diagnoses, however, are being made today than in the past. Exactly why this is so isn't fully understood or known. It is speculated that the rise in autism diagnoses has more to do with our better diagnostic methods and the awareness itself of autism. The diagnosis of autism has expanded to include many spectrum disorders, which encompass more symptoms and conditions, and thus more cases.

So what is autism? Is it a disorder? A condition? A disease? A syndrome? A disability? A challenge? What should we call it? I'm pretty sure no matter what I decide to call "it", my word will be scrutinized by those with very strong opinions of what it is and what it is not. It's actually all of the above. It's not one thing; it's many. It's more than just a word I drop into my Google search engine once a day just for kicks. What concerns me is *my* statistic—1 out of 2 = 50% of my children is affected with ASD, and 100% of my family suffers autism's devastating effects.

There are a few guarantees to expect when you've been given an autism diagnosis. 1.) It's not going to be easy. 2.) It will tax your relationships, almost all of them. 3.) Your life will never be the same again.

At 13 months, I knew there was something off with Dominic. I spent hours online Googling symptoms of autism. Half of the results of typical autism symptoms Dominic exhibited, but then there were several he did not have which always gave me a sense of false hope.

ASD encompasses varying degrees of symptoms and issues and a multitude of combinations of things associated with it. Not to bog you down with autism jargon, but basically there are a few frequently referred to levels of autism that you'll hear people speak of—

High Functioning (Aspberger's would fall into this category.)
Low Functioning or Classic
PDD – NOS – Pervasive Development Disorder/Not Otherwise Specified (We know there is something wrong but we have no idea what to tell you. So, we came up with this name to confuse you.)
ADD Sensory Processing Disorder

Since Dominic was given the PDD-NOS diagnosis, the experts knew something was off but kept telling me when I'd ask, "It can go either way. It can get better or it can get worse." As vague as the diagnosis was, the prognosis was equally as vague.

In Dominic's case, it got worse. And worse. And worse. And his autism is still getting worse as he gets older. I don't have grand thoughts of my son being cured. I don't pretend that I can see a light at the end of the tunnel because we're on a runaway short bus with no stops on the horizon.

In my naivety I had thought that as Dominic got older, he would catch up. We would have a breakthrough, and he would talk or write or go potty on the toilet or dress himself or sleep by himself and be more independent. Instead, as he gets older, he becomes farther and farther behind in his development.

When Dominic was two years old and wasn't talking, I had huge hopes that he would be a late talker. Now I am being told by the speech therapists that he will probably never speak. How can I stay hopeful and positive when I get that kind of news? When I say my son is nonverbal, that means he has no words. Zero. Nada. You'd be amazed at how often people still try to hold a conversation with Dominic, even after I just get done explaining that he is nonverbal. They ask him questions, waiting for his answers. This leads me to believe that people are either not listening or do not believe me and need proof, or are ignorant about autism and what nonverbal means.

EPILEPSY

Not that I'm keeping score, but the epilepsy is kicking the autism's ass! According to www.autismkey.com 25% of kids with ASD have or will have a seizure before the onset of puberty. Epilepsy is prevalent in 10%-30% of those who have been diagnosed with ASD.

After the autism diagnosis, just when I thought it couldn't get worse, at 2 ½ years old, Dominic began having numerous grand mal seizures per day— the heartbreaking violent kind of seizure no one should ever have to watch someone they love experience. Since then, Dominic has had increasingly more and more seizures and has been experiencing different kinds of seizures, such as staring seizures, head-drop seizures, along with the big ones. He's been to four neurologists and had every test imaginable done, and they cannot figure out the cause. The doctors continue to up his dosage of medicines and add new medications, which for the moment, are working to control the majority of seizures. With all of the prescription combinations and trouble-shooting, I can now add Pharmaceutical Trials Administrator to my resume.

For safety, Dominic had to start wearing a helmet anytime he was down on the floor and not on the bed. At first he hated it. But now, he doesn't cry and fight me anymore. He's completely used to it. I ask him when he wants to get down and play, "OK, what do we have to put on first?" and he points to his head. He's been through multiple helmets over the years since he's fallen and hit his head so hard, so many times, that the plastic busts apart often and we have to get a new helmet.

When Dominic gets sick the seizure activity goes up. In our house, fevers = seizures in our already seizure-prone child. The problem with seizures is that they feed off themselves, the more seizures your brain has, the more it's going to have. They multiply like spores, and they mirror each other. So, if you start with seizures on one side of the brain, the other side begins to copy it and then you have an impossible chain reaction. Sigh.

I used to be able to determine the kind of day I was going to have based on how many seizures Dominic would have before 9:00 a.m. Those days I could not put him down, even with his helmet on. You cannot predict when a seizure will come. They just come. And come. And come. And unfortunately, things you cannot control like autistic meltdowns can be culprits.

What's worse is when the cycle includes having severe non-verbal autism.

Here's the irony of it all—

FACT: The more seizures you have, the more you are going to have. (This is why the doctors have tried and continue to try every anti-seizure drug they can think of.)

FACT: You will have more seizures in the heat or if you get overheated. (I have to keep a hot, sweaty helmet on Dominic most of the day. Since the heat from your body escapes from your head, heat is trapped by the helmet. If Dominic gets too hot, he will not sleep or take a nap. Lack of sleep is a main cause of seizures. He has no hope of escaping this vicious cycle.)

FACT: Getting really upset can cause seizures. (Dominic can easily cry or scream himself into a seizure, especially when he holds his breath.)

FACT: Sometimes the side effects of the drugs are worse than the actual seizures. They can range from blurred vision, loss of balance, loss of speech, headaches, nausea, diarrhea, agitation, night terrors, to other types of seizures, insomnia, and more.

FACT: Having seizures all day long prevents a child from cognitive development. If their brains are constantly misfiring, it is almost impossible to teach them new things.

FACT: Seizures preclude walking, running, and climbing. Muscle tone, balance, coordination, and motor skills suffer. Most toddlers with this type of epilepsy regress terribly.

Seizures are cruel, debilitating and senseless and I am growing to hate them more and more with every breath I take. Please don't tell me that God has a plan or that there is a reason for everything or that I am here to learn something from this. There is nothing harder than watching my beautiful, innocent little boy suffer all day long and live inside this vicious, ironic cycle he can't get free from.

I think I would take the autism over the epilepsy any day. I used to curse the autism and then came along its crazy, vindictive cousin, epilepsy. I look back on the early days of Dominic's "autism only" phase of life and wish it were that simple. I remind my husband that "those were the days." I used to love Facebook, Amazon and Pinterest, but now my favorite go-to website is www.epilepsy.com.

> *"Epilepsy is not a disease in and of itself;*
> *it is a symptom of a disease."*
> —Dr. W.W. Sutherling

SEIZURE SAVVY

I am reading as much information as I can to learn more about epilepsy. In the process I am hearing from verbal, neuro-typical people who have epilepsy and parents of children with epilepsy that the side effects from the medicine are almost worse than the actual seizures. I'm gathering plenty of contradicting information that people suffering from the disease are self-medicating. They often wean themselves off of the multiple drugs that their trusted doctors have put them on because when on more than one anti-seizure drug, they actually have more seizures, not fewer.

The more prescriptions they put Dominic on, the worse he would get, cognitively, behavior-wise, motor-skills-wise and seizure-wise. Apparently, these drugs were tested as "stand alone" drugs. They were not meant to be combined with other similar drugs. Some anti-seizure medicines can actually **cause** seizures. The pharmaceutical company of these medications list seizures on their side effects warnings. More shocking to me is that the FDA hasn't even approved many of these anti-seizure drugs for children; they have only been tested and approved for adults.

Dominic was prescribed eight different anticonvulsant drugs in four months by four different doctors. I have to ask myself why these doctors cannot agree or come to a consensus on which anti-seizure medicine to use. Why in the world would they even think to combine four different drugs at once for a toddler?

One time in the hospital, I listened intently as our pediatrician and neurologist argued about whether to give Dominic Phenobarbital. The pediatrician said he prescribed it for his patients and has for many years with no adverse reactions while the neurologist said it was obsolete and a "poison." The neurologist then prescribed Trileptal and Keppra instead.

To them, it was just a discussion about a drug. To me, it was a lesson in "who the hell knows." In the past couple of years, another drug, Topomax, has been added to Dominic's list, making it nine total. Some of the medications we have tried are: Trileptal, Keppra, Lamictal, Clonazepam, Phenobarbital, Depakote, Zonisamide, and Diastat. If you read the warning literature, all of these medicines have unbearable, potentially devastating side effects. For example, Depakote in some instances/patients causes a deadly, irreparable liver reaction leading to death. I had to consider the risk of giving Dominic the Depakote in hopes it was going to stop the seizures and then make deals with God to please not let the Depakote kill him.

Dominic was already a high-strung, high-maintenance child with numerous quirks. He was already fussy and clingy. He was already OCD and ADHD. He already could not focus. He already had poor balance. It seems, these anticonvulsant drugs have magnified these behaviors ten-fold, and they haven't worked 100% to stop the seizures. Since his behavior has gotten consistently worse over the years, guess what the neurologist decided to do? Prescribe another drug—Resperidol for Dominic's horrific behavior.

If I take just one Claritin D for my allergies, it totally changes my sunny disposition; it makes me on edge. If I take a Benedryl, it knocks me out. One Xanax and I don't remember a thing, including my name. I cannot imagine how being on any combination of major anticonvulsant medications at once would affect me. Dominic was taking these medications, sometimes four at a time, and he was just two years old and weighed 30 pounds. How could I help but feel as though I was poisoning my son and contributing to the problem?

When there is a break in the seizures, I get a false sense of security. I assume that the medicine might actually be working or that the seizures have run their course. When you do find a med that's effective, you worry about the medication losing its potency. It's easy for the brain to get used to the drugs and become immune to them. Sigh.

Dominic's current anti-seizure cocktail of choice that he takes twice a day is mostly working for now. It's a combination of the maximum dosage of Depakote and tiny dose of Keppra. Every night while sleeping, however, he screams out and stiffens his body. His eyes usually roll back in his head, and he wakes up for a minute or two and usually goes back to sleep like nothing ever happened. So, I'm wondering what's really going on with these drugs. Are these break-through seizures? Is the medicine not working all the way? Is it just a matter of time before it stops working altogether? Ask our neurologist and all I get is a trivializing shrug and a "hmmmm, interesting…those could be seizures."

Sigh.

One thing is for sure, Dominic hit the jackpot in the seizure department since he gets all of the different types of seizures—

Tonic Clonic – grand mal seizure
Atonic – drop seizure
Myclonic – jerky type of seizure
Absence – spaced out, unaware, gone type of seizure
Primary Generalized Seizures
Tonic Seizures
Clonic Seizures
Partial Seizures
Simple Partial Seizures

Complex partial Seizures
Secondarily Generalized Seizures

Even though it wouldn't matter one bit or change things, I would sure love to know what caused these neurological issues with my son. Pinpointing the cause of epilepsy can be difficult at any age. **In seven out of ten cases, there is no known cause, and it can be labeled as having "idiopathic" epilepsy. "Idiopathic" is a Latin word meaning "of unknown cause." We are idiopathic.**

Here's the rundown of a typical bad day: Dominic wakes up around 4:00 a.m. to 5:00 a.m. with a grand mal seizure that lasts between two and three minutes. When the seizure is over, Dom takes a deep breath, coughs and then passes out from exhaustion. I used to scream and cry and run around the house trying to revive his unresponsive body until I was told it's better to keep him safe and let him sleep.

I have been told that the energy expended in a bad seizure is equivalent to your body running a triathlon! After a seizure, I get the Tylenol ready because a grand mal seizure almost always produces a severe headache and muscle aches. In a normal world, I could simply ask my son how he feels after a seizure or what he needs. In my autism/ epileptic world, I have to guess.

LIVING WITH A TERRORIST

Living with epilepsy is similar to living with a terrorist. It is a form of terrorism. With no warning, once the seizure strikes, you are completely helpless, scared, and confused. You'd do anything for the seizure to stop. You pray, making desperate deals with God. You watch the clock and time it. Once it finally stops, you are hopeful that it will not return. Then the seizure returns and your hopes have been crushed. There is nothing you can do but try to keep your child safe and wait for the return of consciousness.

Even when the seizure activity subsides for a while, you don't stop thinking about when the next one might be coming. You want to be prepared, or as prepared as you can be for something unknown. You spend the rest of your day, week, or month waiting and watching for the seizure to return. You can't relax. Even if the seizures have gone away for a few hours or days, you know they are coming back, planning their attack at the perfect and unsuspecting time when they will inflict the most terror, damage, and pain. This type of terrorist is not concerned with age or innocence; it does not discriminate. It leaves bodily injury, brain cell destruction, and confusion in its path.

You cannot rest living with this terrorist called epilepsy. It's all you can think about. Even when you aren't thinking about it, you are thinking about it. Things are no longer up to you. You have no control over the situation, timing, length or severity of the seizure. The epilepsy terrorist feeds on your despair and anxiety while you wait for the other shoe to drop. You are merely its unwilling hostage. Dominic and our entire family are living in a war zone, suffering from PTSD.

I still don't know which seizures are worse, the big ass-kicking seizures or the quick drop-you-to-the-floor seizures. How long will I have to sleep with one eye open as I listen to the breathing patterns and carefully monitor any jerking motion of Dominic's body in the gleam of our night light?

Never before did I imagine that I would become an epilepsy expert. Forget about the autism, I feel as though I've gotten a crash course in seizures over the last five years. My daily vocabulary includes words like Electroencephalogram (EEG), cortex, postictal, atonic, myoclonic, and tonic-clonic. The autism is merciless, the epilepsy is beyond cruel.

As a parent you want nothing more than your children to grow up happy, healthy and well rounded with a strong moral compass; but mostly **healthy**. People don't realize what a serious and disabling disease epilepsy is. I never gave two shits about it before, yet it affects more than two million people. It affects my beautiful boy, and my heart breaks silently a little more with each seizure.

THE AUTISM/EPILEPSY SANDWICH

I keep getting asked about epilepsy and Dominic's diagnosis and prognosis— what it means, what he has, how long he'll have it, what caused it? Which came first the chicken or the egg? Did the autism contribute to the epilepsy, or has the epilepsy contributed to the autism? They're a little like peanut butter and jelly; they just go together, and no one really knows why.

While epilepsy can begin at any time of life, 50 percent of all cases begin before the age of 25. Many seizure disorders start in early childhood because immature brains are more susceptible to malfunctions, no matter what the cause.

There is a multitude of possible causes in children. These include problems with brain development before birth, lack of oxygen during or following birth, a head injury that leaves scarring on the brain, unusual structures in the brain, tumors, a prolonged fever, or the after-effects of severe brain infections such as meningitis or encephalitis. When a cause can be identified, these children are labeled as having symptomatic epilepsy.

Since we live a couple of hours from Stanford University Medical Center, we were referred by our Santa Rosa Neurologist and decided to go to this world-renowned hospital for help and a sleep study EEG. Some of the doctors and nurses we encountered were the best of the best, but many could stand to take a refresher course in Bedside Manners 101. They didn't have much compassion, especially when dealing with an autistic child. I was wishing they would check their giant medical egos at the door when talking to distraught parents at their wits'-freaking end.

We also received a referral to a pediatric neurologist at the University of California of San Francisco (UCSF), another cutting-edge hospital. It was unfortunate, however, that the staff at Stanford was a little put-off because they knew we were going to UCSF for our epilepsy treatment; maybe it was my imagination but it seemed these two hospitals might be somewhat competitive with each other.

One of the nurse practitioners at Stanford asked me what my goal was going to UCSF; which I thought was the oddest question ever. I told her that obviously my goal was to get Dominic's seizures under control by consulting with a pediatric neurologist. I told her I was hoping there might be a surgical procedure to reduce the amount of seizures. She quickly dismissed that idea by telling me that Dominic would not be a candidate based on his type of generalized seizures.

We talked further about the genetic testing that had been done for Fragile X, Angelmen's Syndrome, and Prodder Willy, all of which had come back normal. At first when I found out that Dominic did not have these genetic disorders, I was ecstatic. But this Stanford nurse practitioner was quick to point out that: just because he doesn't have one of those genetic diseases, he probably still has some form of DNA corruption and that he'll have to continue being tested for other disorders. If those come back normal, that wouldn't necessarily indicate good news because it would only mean there isn't a genetic test that exists yet to determine what Dominic actually has! In other words, getting negative genetic testing results does not necessarily mean anything positive.

Sigh.

Then all hell broke loose, and hell hath no fury like a seizure. Dominic was having 40-60 head-drop seizures a day, the grand mals were not as frequent, yet, but by far, harder to witness. His high score was four grand mals in one day, until one warm summer day in July 2009 when Dominic had nine grand mal seizures in six hours by noontime. They were coming almost every hour and didn't stop. We called UCSF and they told us to go to our local hospital to see if they could control them. Two doses of Ativan did nothing but wire him. Dominic was still wide awake and continuing to have more grand mals. We found out the hard way that some barbiturate type of medicines actually have an opposite, paradoxal effect on him.

We thought our local hospital was going to transport Dominic to UCSF because they didn't have a pediatric neurologist on staff, but UCSF declined. They said there was nothing they could do for us there that they couldn't do locally. Basically, there is nothing you can do for seizures except watch, wait, and keep the individual safe while trying to find a blend of anti-seizure medications that work to control them.

Dominic continued to have more seizures during our hospital stay while we watched multiple reruns of *Dora and the Wishing Star*. I had some wishes of my own for Dora, like shut the &%$# up! That little girl can talk. Dominic had 12 grand mals in 20 hours.

Finally he went to sleep, but he woke up cranky and hung-over from the drugs. Suddenly he had another grand mal seizure. After 45 seconds the nurse was screaming for someone to bring her a shot of Ativan STAT. (I kept waiting for her to grab the crash cart and paddles like I'd seen in TV doctor shows.) This seizure barely lasted a minute when Dominic came out of it. He was lying on his side, coming out of the seizure and she was still asking for the shot.

I said, "Uhm, excuse me. You are not going to give him that Ativan again are you?"

And she said, "Yes!"

And I said, "No! He stopped seizing. He doesn't need it."

She said, "No, he's still seizing and it's almost been two minutes."

And so I argued, "No. He's not. I've seen him have almost 100 of these now and he's done."

She said, "No. He's not responding…"

And then I lost it. In my best, most stern and composed voice I could muster since I hadn't slept for 48 hours, I said, "No! You don't get it. He's always out of it after a big seizure. He's textbook postictal. It's what happens after he has a grand mal!"

I couldn't believe I was talking to a nurse. Had she skipped that day in nursing school? Was this her first day on the job?

She told me since his eyes were rolled back when she lifted his eyelids, he was still seizing. Then we argued some more. I told her we needed another opinion before she jabbed him with a dose of a benzodiazepine, which was going to have the opposite effect on him than she wanted.

She put the syringe down by her over-zealous side and called for the nurse supervisor. The nurse supervisor came in quickly and asked, "What's going on?"

The stab-happy nurse armed with the shot said, "He is still seizing and I need to give him this Ativan, but this mother won't let me."

The Supervisor Nurse examined him. "He's not seizing anymore," she said. "He doesn't need that."

With great relief, I said, "Thank you. No more shit and giggles narcotics, please. I can't get through another day and night like yesterday."

The stab-happy nurse immediately got defensive. She tried to over explain why she thought he was still seizing. I just held my little son, as I always do, and told him everything was going to be all right.

Not one second goes by in any given day when I am not worried about Dominic's seizures. It's the worst, most sickening feeling I have ever had in my whole entire life. It's a helpless feeling that I cannot describe, other than to compare it to that of living in constant fear. When he's at school or someone is babysitting him and I get a call on my cell phone my heart literally stops beating.

Just like autism, the worst part about epilepsy is that it is individually based. Like fingerprints, no two cases are exactly alike. It affects each person differently and to varying degrees. There are different causes and triggers for everyone and with that, each individual responds differently to the medications. So I will continue looking for answers, relying on doctors and prescriptions, and my favorite all-time activity—waiting and worrying.

THE C WORD

Once you've known someone with cancer, it's harder to say the word without thinking about that person or people. Even though I don't like to think about it, I notice that it's always been in the back of my mind somewhere that I would get it or someone I love would get it.

Our family has never had a history of cancer. Heart disease and diabetes, yes. Cancer? No. Then 7 years ago my mom got the bad news. She was diagnosed with breast cancer and is now our family history of cancer. We were lucky, for the time being, she had a lumpectomy went through chemo and radiation and was given a clean bill of health. Fast forward to 2 years ago. On her 5 year anniversary of being "cancer free", my mom got the bad news that her cancer was back and had spread. They started treatment immediately—she was first put into a pharmaceutical study which sounded promising. We all had high hopes. One of the conditions of participating in a research study like that is that your cancer cannot worsen or spread or they kick you out of the study. My mom was kicked out. She went in for one of her full body scans and the results came back with additional "spots" on her liver. So besides being excused from the study, she had to deal with her cancer spreading.

They put her on permanent continual chemo treatment. The doctors decided it best not to remove the cancer but to treat the entire body instead with chemo for the rest of her life. It's hard to stay positive when surrounded by so much gloom.

Have you ever cried so much, you have no more tears left?

The autism came along and shook me to my core—it became all I ate, drank, slept and breathed. Then came the aggressive epilepsy which kicked my ass and made me long for the simpler days of just the autism. I guess I was served the side of epilepsy and a mom with breast cancer in an attempt to prepare me for the absolute worst day of my life, Dominic's Cancer scare.

What are the odds Dominic would have a triple threat: Autism, Epilepsy and probable Cancer?

The New York Times released an article on August 13, 2013 called ***Autism's Unexpected Link to Cancer Genes: As surprised researchers have discovered, some people with autism have mutated cancer or tumor genes that apparently caused their brain disorder.*** Jonathan Sebat, chief of the Center for Molecular Genomics of Neuropsychiatric Diseases at the University of California, San Diego, has described the parallels between cancer and autism as "quite uncanny." We're used to sickness in our family. Dominic has been sick with upper respiratory illnesses his entire life. I've gotten really good at being able to determine when it's time to take him to the doctor, or so I thought. He constantly had colds and flues and bronchitis-type of infections and viruses. He's also been known to have weird oxygen and breathing issues since he was born, including the sleep apnea.

When Dominic first starting having seizures and they looked at his history of illnesses at 2 ½ years old, they decided to remove his tonsils and over-sized adenoids. The doctors thought this would help with his illnesses, breathing, oxygen intake, seizures and sleep apnea. So at the urging of the doctors, we had them removed.

The surgery didn't help. Dominic continued to fight illness. Once in preschool, he would catch everything. He was constantly sick and the seizure activity only got worse. He obviously had a weak immune system. We spent many nights in the emergency room after hearing from the Pediatrician that Dominic had a virus and there was nothing they could do.

After dozens of appointments with the Pediatricians, and asking why he was so sick all the time, the Pediatrician would attribute the sicknesses to being a "school age" kid and send us home. This went on for two years. From age 5-7 Dominic missed over 100 days of school from being sick. Each time I would take Dominic to the Pediatrician, I would be sent home with an eye roll and the instructions on how to alternate Tylenol and Motrin to control the fevers and make him more comfortable while he was sick.

Dominic's illnesses were coming every 4-6 weeks like clockwork. Why was I the only one who was concerned with this pattern? Doctors continued to argue with me that it was "normal" for a child to be sick this often since he was going to school. I would lament over the symptoms with the doctor and ask them if they felt it was coincidentally odd that Dominic was sick every month with the SAME exact symptoms; a high fever and upper respiratory issues.

Not believing the first Pediatrician, I moved on to Pediatrician #2. I was told the same thing from Pediatrician #2…"Your son has a virus". Pediatrician #2 wasn't nice about it—nor would he tolerate my crazy theories about what might be causing Dominic's persistent fevers. From my Googling and Web MD research, I actually found something called Persistent Fever Syndrome. Did he like that I was printing things out and bringing in my own diagnosis? No. He brushed off my many possible diagnoses I had found including:

Lupus
Cancer
Multiple Sclerosis
Persistent Fever Syndrome

After 12 days of a high fever spiking at 103 degrees and after alternating the Tylenol and Motrin around the clock, Dominic wasn't showing any signs of improvement. He was miserable and the worst part is he wasn't sleeping.

Jim and I went through 9 days of pure hell—trying to get Dominic to lay down and go to sleep. He would sleep for 10-15 minutes and then jolt himself awake. He was exhausted and we were exhausted. I was at my wits end and I really thought we were never going to get 2 or 3 hours of sleep ever again. Besides being wide awake, he was miserable and crying and mostly pointed to his head as if he was in a great deal of pain.

I made another appointment with, yet, another Pediatrician, this would be Pediatrician #3. It was a Friday and day 12 of Dominic's high fever. I took Dominic into his appointment and as nice as the doctor was, he also told me it was a "virus". During the appointment, Dominic's fever had broken—we had been through at least 3 bottles of Tylenol and Motrin over the last 12 days. I went through my rundown of diagnosis with the new doctor and he blew them all out of the water except for the Persistent Fever Syndrome. Winner! Winner! Chicken Dinner! I thought we finally cracked the case. He told me he would refer us to an Immunologist and Rheumatologist at UCSF. I couldn't have been happier. Finally, I thought, we were going to have the answers. While we were there, I specifically asked this Doctor if he thought Dominic could have Cancer—Hodgkin's or Lymphoma since those frequently came up on my Web MD searches. He assured me NO. He checked Dominic's lymph nodes and said that his spleen was not enlarged. No blood tests or anything else were ordered. He sent us home with the Tylenol and Motrin regimen and that was that. He told me just because Dominic was pointing to his head and crying meant nothing. He said kids his age point to their heads when they hurt in other parts of the body which I had a hard time believing. I said, "Really, because when he stubs his toe or has a hangnail, he doesn't point to his head. He points to the place where it hurts." He was adamant about this and thought he would really convince by telling me, "Yes, even normal children don't always point to the correct place and they're "smart". Hmph. Really nice, my son is autistic, he's not a moron. He can point to what hurts I wanted to scream! Doctor #3 had just completely offended me and I wasn't sure if it was intentional or not.

Dominic never got better. All weekend, he fought a high fever. I was getting so frustrated because there was absolutely nothing I could do other than force the Tylenol and Motrin on him. Still, he wasn't sleeping. We tried sleeping him in his little recliner in front of the TV since he seemed most comfortable there. Still, no sleep.

Monday came and I called the new Pediatrician #3 again. I told him Dominic was still sick, not sleeping and had a high fever. We were on day 15 now of fevers and no sleep, even I know there is something gravely wrong with that and I'm no Doctor.

He told me it wasn't unusual for these "summertime viruses" to last 15 days and dismissed me again, never asking to see Dominic again for any kind of follow up. At this point I felt like a woman without an island. I emailed Dominic's neurologist at UCSF hoping he would take an interest in Dominic's case since the fever, no sleep and headaches had become the worst of the mystery "virus" and were now his seizure control was an issue. I was also curious why our Neurologist at UCSF had never felt it necessary to refer us to any specialists at UCSF, knowing Dom's issues and symptoms and why did this brand new Doctor feel it was necessary. I thought I could get to the Immunologist and Rheumatologist faster and more efficiently if referred by our in-house UCSF Neurologist but what do I know? I'm just an annoying, demanding mom with a penchant to Google everything. He flat out refused. He also quickly dismissed the pointing to the head as any neurological concern, again, even after it had now been documented for over a year. I tried not taking things too personally but felt instantly rebuffed.

At a complete loss, I finally took Dominic to the Emergency Room at our local hospital. The first thing they do is triage and determine how severe your "injury/illness" is. They began with Dominic's temperature, it was 103 degrees. He looked very pale and had a very high respiratory rate.

When they put the little gadget on his finger for his oxygen saturation, it was extremely low, in the 70's. They kept insisting that there must be something wrong with their gadget and they tried another, same thing. I tried telling them that he always has a low oxygen saturation level when they use his fingers—but they didn't listen. They kept insisting it was a defective machine. Finally, I got a nurse to try the gadget on his toe. Yep. When the oxygen gadget is on his toe his rate went into the high 80's. Still low, but better.

The first thing the doctor did was order a blood panel—and a chest x-ray. Dominic's white blood count was low which was some cause for concern but more concerning was his chest x-ray. The ER Doctor came back to the room to give us the results of Dom's chest x-ray. I wasn't worried; after all, it was a virus! I thought they were just doing the chest x-ray so that they could say they did one and charge us the very reasonable emergency room cost of $3,000.

My heart sunk when I heard the news. Dom had a large mass the size of a small orange in the center of his chest, pressing on his lungs. When the doctor said mass all I could hear was cancer. She said there was a chance it could be pneumonia and a weird defect in the film. I never thought I would wish for pneumonia for one of my kids but consider the alternative—Cancer.

The next step was that they needed to be sure what the mass was and the only way to really be sure would be to do an MRI of his chest. Easier said than done—Dominic would surely not hold still for 30 seconds, let alone 10-15 minutes, so he had to be sedated. Sedation is no big deal right? It is if you have a seizure disorder and pneumonia. Let the nightmare begin!

The results came back and the doctor sat me down and told me the bad news. Dominic did, in fact, have a large tumor in his chest. The tumor is what had been causing the pneumonia because it was crushing one of his lungs and the infection in his lung had been there for a very long time and because of the tumor the infection couldn't get out—perhaps 18 months or so. This tumor and pneumonia would surely account for his recurring and persistent monthly fevers that had plagued him which three Pediatricians wrote off as a "virus". My faith in the medical field was quickly fading.

I had so many questions. How long had this tumor been there? Why did none of the doctors take the time to do a blood test or chest x-ray after the numerous office visits, phone calls and repeat visits of the same illness? Had this been a typical, verbal child, it would have been so much easier to detect. All I would have had to do is ask my son, "What is wrong? Or where does it hurt? Surely, I would have been told, "My chest hurts mommy, I can't breathe very well. Help me." If he was neuro-typical and could talk, perhaps even a Pediatrician would have taken his illnesses more seriously instead of assuming I was an over-reacting mother with hypochondria tendencies.

Along with the countless questions I finally had answers. This had to be why he couldn't sleep. This had to be causing the pain in back, head and neck and why he would cry and point to his head constantly. Besides the fever, he must have been so uncomfortable, especially when laying down flat on his back. No wonder he could never lay still, relax and go to sleep! I felt like the worst mom ever. I had yelled at him several times in my fits of pure exhaustion in the middle of night to Lay Down and Go to Sleep!!! I had been so frustrated with him, despite him being sick. I was getting weary and tired of the constant crying and pointing to his head. I was struggling and exhausted. He was doing it so often that we started to think it was just out of habit for our attention.

It was around 7:00 pm, we had been in the emergency room for the better part of the day. Jim was at home with Jimmy and on his way to the ER. He first entered the exam room by himself. He must have been able to read the look of complete shock on my swollen and reddened face. "Shut the door, I have to talk to you", I whispered. And then I lost it.

Dominic was still pretty out of it from the sedation. I still wonder if he understands everything we talk about in his presence. Sometimes I forget that I need to be careful about what I say in front of him. I get confused about his comprehension based on him being nonverbal, we really don't know all that he understands.

I told Jim that our worst fear in the universe had come true, a fear we had talked about and imagined…one of our kids had a tumor and it was likely cancer. He gave me a long, hard hug and we cried. I could not imagine getting through the next ten minutes, let alone the next few weeks, months or years if we were that lucky.

The doctor came back in to let me know the next course of action. They had called UCSF and we were waiting transport to UCSF in an ambulance. I couldn't recognize what the emergency was because I didn't fully understand the gravity of the situation. I asked why can't we go to UCSF tomorrow (the next morning)? I told them I would drive him there first thing. They said the nature and location of the tumor was seriously impacting his breathing, he had pneumonia and may not make it through the night. I felt like the worst mom ever, how could I let this happen to my son?

We waited what seemed like an eternity for the ambulance and we finally arrived at UCSF around 11:00pm. Dominic was exhausted as was I. Little did I know or remember how unsettling and un-restful it is to be in the hospital. Between the constant fluids, medicine, ivs, and vitals going on, Dominic was never allowed to sleep more than an hour here or there. All night long I had different teams of Doctors coming in to interview me about Dominic and his health history.

The first doctor to greet us was unbelievably nice and gorgeous, as in Dr. McDreamy gorgeous. I thought what a great strategy they had putting him in charge of the greeting and formalities. He was the on-call Fellow in the Children's Pediatric Oncology. He first put my mind to ease letting me know that they had looked at the MRI and thought it was a Teratoma (germ cell) tumor and I was relieved to learn that this type of tumor was the "best" type of tumor to get if you are going to get a tumor…he said a lot of the Teratoma tumors were benign. The plan of action was going to be fairly straight forward. They would go in and remove the tumor, send it off to pathology and if the tumor did not have any embryonic cells and was a "mature" Teratoma, then we would be done. If the tumor had the embryonic cells, that would be a malignant form of cancer and Dominic would require many months of treatment such as chemotherapy.

A couple of hours later, Dr. McDreamy returned. He told me he may have misspoken because they had been looking at Dominic's blood under a microscope and had found abnormalities which were consistent with Leukemia or another type of cancer. I swallowed what was left of my hope. Gulp.

The next two days were crazy. We had several teams of doctors coming in and out of the room with conflicting updates. UCSF is a teaching and research hospital with interns and residents all over the place jockeying for their turn at a great case. It was like an episode out of Grey's Anatomy. The surgery team wanted to operate immediately, the oncology team wanted to do a biopsy and treat it with chemo and radiation. The anesthesiology team was with the surgery team and they had already reserved an operating room for Friday morning. Just when I thought they were going to remove the tumor, another team would come in and tell me that they were not going to remove it because it could make things worse.

The doctors all finally got together at some point and came to an agreement to remove the tumor. Surgery was set for 7:30 am. Sure it was early, but we weren't sleeping anyway. Besides all the paperwork I had to fill out and the release of liability waivers and warnings about blood transfusions, etc. We were lucky that it was all happening so quickly. It didn't give me much time to dwell. I had so many people in and out of the room I didn't have time to fall apart and worry. This was no minor surgery. Because of the location of the tumor, they had to saw his sternum in half and go into his chest cavity just like they were performing open heart surgery—except they weren't touching the heart. They also weren't sure exactly how badly the tumor had attached itself to the lung and whether or not they could save the lung. By and large they don't like to perform surgery on a patient that already has an infection/ pneumonia. It was a highly dangerous surgery for a 7 year old.

Dominic's surgery turned out fine. No issues to speak of other than an 8" scar down the middle of his chest, from his collar bone down to his navel. We remained in ICU for recovery until his pneumonia cleared. They kept him on a serious regimen of antibiotics. His lungs filled with even more fluid after the surgery so they continued to give him Lasix to pee out the fluids and they did several chest x-rays daily. Finally his fever broke and they put us in a regular room. Being autistic, Dominic wasn't the easiest patient. He's also pretty active and not used to being tied to a bed with so many IV's. It was all we could do to keep him from ripping out the IVs and chest tubes. The more alert he became, the harder it was to control his behavior. Besides sitting on his legs and restraining his arms, there was little we could do. They didn't want to keep him sedated and cut his pain medication off after 48 hours. Since Dominic can't talk and was so agitated, I had no way to know how much pain he really was in.

One of the hardest things about the surgery was the waiting and worrying about the pathology results. I had so much time to sit and re-evaluate my life from that crowded hospital room. I went through every emotion imaginable in such a short period of time. At first I was angry. Angry at God, if there is one, because how could he do this to a small, innocent child? I've been angry for years now. If I'm going to be completely honest, I have had anger issues with God and issues with my faith since Dominic was first diagnosed with Autism. With each set back, delay and health issue, I've felt tested and pushed to the darkest depths of despair and I felt very alone as I cursed Him in the darkness, my darkness.

I was angry because I felt Dominic had really drawn the short-stick in this life and with the autism issues and then the epilepsy and brain issues, it just wasn't fair. As hard of a child Dominic is sometimes, I could not imagine my life without him. He's weaved into our daily fabric of life and the challenges, meltdowns, struggles and his small triumphs are all part of our day.

I was sad, worried and more depressed than I have ever been before. I had just gone on antidepressants a few weeks before the cancer scare and since I didn't feel like they were working I went off them two days before Dominic's visit to the ER. Timing hasn't always been my strong suit. I felt like I was being taught a lesson—for being such a whiney little bitch about the autism. It was like someone in charge was saying to me, "Oh yeah…you think the autism and epilepsy is bad, how about this?"

It took 7 excruciating, anxiety-filled days to get the pathology results. Each time the Oncology team would come in I thought they were there to deliver the news. On Friday, 10 days into our stay, we were given the news that the Teratoma tumor was benign and was made up of mature cells! It was the best news I have ever heard in my whole life. I thanked God and apologized for my harsh words spoken in anger.

It seems every time we get good news and take a step forward, we end up getting bad news and take a couple of steps back. Three months after his tumor removal, at a follow up Cat Scan at UCSF, we received more scary news. Dominic has white spots on his lungs and they don't know what they are. He wasn't sick with any kind of respiratory issues which means it could be another type of infection, bacteria, fungus, scar tissue, lung disease or cancer. Can we never get a straight answer? Dominic is a medical mystery. Now we just wait while they continue to do Cat Scans every couple of months to determine if the spots are growing. What is said to cause cancer? Ahhhh, yes, exposure to radiation. What are we doing to his little body every single time we x-ray or scan him? We do not know what those lung spots portend for Dominic.

This recent cancer scare changed me. It changed my mind set about autism and priorities. It took Dominic getting a tumor to prove to me how second and third the autism really is when we're talking about life or death. Does it really matter that Dominic is developmentally delayed, socially challenged and nonverbal? Does it really matter that he rides a short bus? Those things when you put them next to a life-threatening condition seem pale in comparison. Of course I still wish for a better life for him but I'm not different than any parent wishing a better life for their children. I always said health and happiness came first—before anything else and I stand by that. As long as Dominic is healthy, I can handle the other stuff. But keeping him healthy and safe has thus far, in his short life, been a test.

I know there are kids out there that have it much worse than Dominic and it breaks my heart. Cancer and other diseases do not discriminate against children or children with special needs or typical children for that matter. Dominic is a brave kid and he's now an official member of the zipper club. The scar on his chest will always be a reminder of how strong he is and all he has endured. Each time I see the 8" scar running down the middle of his chest it's a stern reminder of how precious life is and how little control we really do have over it.

GENETICS

I was 38 years old and my husband 49 when we got pregnant with Dominic. Because of my age, we had all of the testing done that we could— the triple test, the amnio, and CVS. Everything came back normal. They have tests for some birth defects including Down

Autism Spectrum Disorder and Beyond | 35

Syndrome but nothing to tell you if your child is going to have autism. I have to ask myself, would I have really wanted to know in advance?

You want your child to be healthy, and you want to be known to have only passed on things like a small waist, long legs, big brown eyes, a high IQ, stunning good looks, and a sense of humor. I rack my brain and wonder what I did when I was pregnant to have caused this. I can't help but feel responsible every single day for Dominic's condition. As much as it sucks for me and for our family to watch Dominic suffer, seizure after unexplainable ffffing seizure, it is the hardest on him. And, he is going to have to live with this condition (according to doctors) for his entire life whether he has a mutant chromosome or not.

Once the autism and epilepsy was diagnosed, they did some extensive genetic testing at Stanford Children's Hospital. Everything they tested for came back normal. I wanted to write a poem about our good news, but I had a hard time finding things to rhyme with chromosome!

TOXINS AND VACCINATIONS

Sometimes the paranoid side of me kicks in and only wants Dominic to eat organic tomatoes. My husband, Jim, was reading a book by Kevin Touhey and has me scared of pesticides, hormones and pretty much anything you might buy at most grocery stores.

I could make myself crazy trying to eliminate anything that might be potentially harmful. We wouldn't be sleeping on a chemical filled mattress emitting toxic gasses while we sleep, or use an antiperspirant, perfume or air freshener.

We'd be living in a toxin-free padded oxygenated room built out of bamboo with a HEPA filter running on solar power eating organic soybeans and drinking heavily filtered water only from glass bottles! Then I get confused because it turns out that the chemicals in manufactured soy could increase the risk of breast cancer in women, brain damage in both men and women, and abnormalities in infants.

Guess what? The only liquid Dominic drank for 4 years was soy milk! How bad do I feel now?

There are reports that toxins in carpet and carpet glue kill rats, cause brain damage and seizures. And, don't forget the toxic BPA and PVC in plastic bottles, including baby bottles, sippy cups, and the drinking water bottles I buy in huge quantities. They can cause cancer and kill brain cells, just like the Teflon in the pots and pans I used for years. I've finally just thrown away all of my Tupperware just in case... Thank God there isn't fracking happening nearby or I'd be worried about that too.

There is the theory that food allergies, red dyes, and yeast are also contributing factors to autism, ADHD, and inappropriate behavior. And, don't forget cell phones, Wifi and emissions of electromagnetic radiation from electronic equipment in the home and workplace. And, here's another concern— jet fuel from planes flying high above us that leak JP-4 and JP-8 fuel chemical compounds into our atmosphere and environment. I could go on and on. Does it bother me that we live in the middle of vineyard? A vineyard that could be potentially harmful and full of pesticides and toxins seeping into our well. We don't drink the well water but we do cook with it and bathe in it.

There's so much information out there to decipher, depending on which article you read or which channel you watch. Too much information is being driven by large pharmaceutical or mass-market conglomerate and media funding which is also politically motivated. It's all a crapshoot. Whom and what can you really trust? And, where could you live and be completely safe from any hazard?

My personal favorite is the debate over vaccinations in children. *The U.S. vaccine schedule has grown from 10 vaccines given to our children in the 1980s to 36 today, perfectly matching the dramatic rise in autism.* Is this all just pure coincidence? Maybe. Maybe not.

Our family is not a non-vaccinating family. It's not my stance that vaccinations cause autism, although I do believe that over-vaccinating an already autism-prone child who may be sick could contribute to autism symptoms and make things worse. Our entire family has been vaccinated. With Dominic's health and seizure history, however, I stopped vaccinating him at 18 months old. It wasn't that I didn't want him to be vaccinated; it was because he was constantly sick with upper respiratory infections, viruses, fevers and then he started having seizures. He was on so many antibiotics as a baby I thought for sure his body had become immune to them.

What happens when you take your child to the doctor for shots and your child has a fever or is ill? They recommend not vaccinating them at that point and send you home to come back when your child is healthy. So, what do you do when your child is never healthy? Do you roll the dice and hope for the best? I just could not put another potentially harmful toxin into Dominic's already sick and weak immune system and give his compromised brain one more thing to process.

I have been intently researching the subject of vaccinating. I can't help but feel that not all kids are created with the same immune system and equipped to handle the same dose and amount of injections. My view is this— vaccinations are a shot in the dark and need to be spread out over time and only given when a child is well enough to receive them.

CHOSEN ONE MY BUTT

Having a child with autism brings new meaning to the term "patience tester," especially when you throw in the stages of the terrible twos, threes, fours, fives, sixes, etc. Taking Dominic out places turns into a side-show that, at first, I was embarrassed by. I couldn't bear the stares and whispers of this "out-of-control" child who did nothing but scream and shake his head back and forth. People don't always understand that

Dominic is different, because at first glance he looks like any other child. His behavior, however, can make him look like the biggest brat you have ever seen.

Taking Dominic out in public can be a serious cause of stress for me. I've fantasized about getting t-shirts made that I could dress him in that would say things like, "Kiss My Aspberger's," "Stop Judging My Mom. I'm Autistic," "This Isn't A Tantrum. I'm On The Spectrum," or "This Tantrum Brought To You By Autism." Then I realize I literally would be putting a label on my child. What kind of mother would I be labeling my child just so people would cut me some slack for his behavior?

Stop telling me that God has a plan for us because I am hard-pressed to understand how a God can plan this for an innocent child and put him through excruciating pain and debilitating seizures. A plan is defined as: *A scheme, program, or method worked out beforehand for the accomplishment of an objective.* What could possibly be God's objective? If Dominic is here to be my "teacher", what does that mean for his life? Was a happy, independent and healthy life sacrificed on my behalf so that I may learn something and Dominic plays the role of a martyr?

I hear these two phrases over and over: "You've been chosen by God to be this boy's mom," and "It's a blessing from above." If you count me watching my child suffer every day with seizures and being a prisoner in his own mind to autism a blessing, then we need to talk. If you count the anxiety, insomnia, panic, and tantrums a blessing, then we need to talk. If you count being nonverbal, severely developmentally delayed and lacking basic independent life skills a blessing, then we need to talk.

I don't share the opinion of many parents with a child with ASD that autism is a gift or blessing, even though Dominic's autism, developmental delays, learning disabilities and the way he processes information have given me the gift of awareness. That's as optimistic as I can get about autism and epilepsy. I am now fully aware.

As a mom I know that my main job is to help my son try to understand his limitations while not being so focused on how other people view me or him. Not caring what people think has been a hurdle for me, and I struggle with it every day.

Most people take for granted that communication skills and learning abilities come naturally. I've had to learn that I can't expect a breakthrough very often, because if I do, I'm only setting myself up for more daily disappointment. I'm new to this world of autism. I don't always know if I should treat Dominic like a "special" child or treat him like I did my other neuro-typical son. These are the things they don't teach you in Economics or American History. Since we don't learn **Parenting a Special Kid 101**, and there are no warning labels and an operating manual, what are parents supposed to do when every day feels like a malfunction? Every day begins to feel like a mistake. I feel more like a failure for not doing enough to help my son than I do about being "chosen" or "blessed." I used to feel guilty about feeling this way, now I don't. My advice to those who feel as I do is the following—

1. Accept your situation for what it is.
2. Take every day one day at a time. Try not to focus on the future, even though that's almost impossible!
3. Do your best to let go of the life you used to have so that you can embrace the life that is now yours.
4. Don't beat yourself up about not doing enough.

"Some people think to be strong is to never feel pain. In reality, the strongest people are those who feel it, understand it, accept and learn from it."
—Author Unknown

NORMAL VS. SPECIAL

There's an online discussion about a completely hypothetical topic that has been popping up on several blogs in the autism community. The debate is about a magic pill that you could give your child to cure autism. The question is if it were available, would you have your child with autism take it?

One woman said she wouldn't give it to her child because it would be too scary (for him) suddenly to be "normal" after being autistic. She continued explaining that "normal" isn't all it's cracked up to be. She went on to enlighten me on how autistic people can lead happy and fulfilling lives. She stated that autistic children are terrific and that autism is beautiful. She didn't feel the need to "fix" her daughter because she already loved her just the way she was.

While I completely respect her opinion, I felt compelled to chime in because this topic really struck a chord with me. First of all, autism is anything but beautiful. Yes, every autistic child's heart, soul, and spirit are beautiful. But to talk about autism as this wonderful and precious gift, I think, is in some way trying to be righteous about it. Autistic children are not the "chosen" ones."

I know that some autistic people live productive lives, but talk to any verbal high-functioning autistic adult, who can put into words what it is like to be autistic, and most will tell you how they cannot self-regulate easily, have problems communicating, experience great feelings of inner turmoil and anxiety, and usually feel out of sync and uneasy in their own skin.

Would I give Dominic a magic pill to cure his autism? ABSOL-FREAKING-LUTELY, without question or hesitation! And, it has nothing to do with loving him any less whether he's autistic or "normal."

As a parent, you want what is best for your child. So, let's reverse the question and ask parents of neuro-typical children this question: If they had the choice, would they give their "normal" child autism?

I'm thinking this question would get an overwhelming and resounding "Hell NO" response.

Autistic children have it harder in school, and low functioning autistic kids and adults struggle with basic life independence. Some autistic people are violent and hurt themselves and others and have no self-control. Some autistic people don't know the feeling of love and can't stand human touch. Some go their entire lives locked inside themselves, trapped. Some autistic people need to be institutionalized. And, I'm just scraping the surface here!

With autism comes a myriad of health issues. Dominic's seizures are part of his severe autism. His coordination, speech, muscle tone, and sleep issues are a factor of the autism. I want to fix him! I'd do anything to fix him! And I am in no way ashamed to say that. Some will argue that there is nothing to fix…that he is not broken. It doesn't make me any less of a mom to want my child to have a fighting chance at life; to be able to go to college, have a home and career or fall in love and have children of his own, if that is what he wants for himself. I want him to have options and unfortunately options do not come with autism.

AWARE ABOUT THE AWARENESS

Autism Awareness Day is April 2nd. Wow! One whole day. Really? And then someone must have gotten the memo at Corporate Autism, Inc. wherein perhaps the autism community should have considered dedicating one entire month to it instead? Maybe they'd seem more compassionate or maybe it's just good business. So, now, April is Autism Awareness month.

Don't get me wrong, I am all for autism awareness. That is the driving force behind writing this book. I want people to be aware of autism as a whole and not some skewed version of living with a card-counting genius or brilliant child on a video—gone viral version of autism.

I want to remind people of the challenges and heartbreak associated with parenting a child with autism. The hard part of autism. The dark side of autism. The autism no one wants to talk about. Do I need a day to contemplate, celebrate and recognize autism one day in April? No. But, beggars can't be choosers. We wanted autism awareness, right?

Some think by acknowledging Autism Awareness Day once a year is all they need to do to feel aware. Changing your Facebook profile picture to BLUE or LIGHT IT UP BLUE are nice gestures and they show a level of "social awareness" albeit but think of the people that live that color blue every single day. For us in the autism trenches, going "blue" is not a mood thing or status update. It's our life. And yay for global autism recognition and for now having an Autism Awareness day but geeeeezuz, every day is autism awareness day at our house. Should I change all of my light bulbs to blue? Is that going to cure Autism? I'm aware. I'm good and aware.

Instead of one day of Autism Awareness, I'd like us parents with children with ASD take one full day OFF of autism and get some global support for that! We can all pretend it doesn't exist, live in a bubble and go back to our lives before autism. That would be nice. I wonder what color that day would be.

THE ASD COMMUNITY

My experience in the autism community has shown me that there are many factions and schisms among the believers who belong to the Church of The Autistic Spectrum. We're a hard bunch to please. I think it's because most of us are so sleep deprived, bitter, and depressed that it's hard to make us happy. It's not surprising when you consider how divided and fractured religions are. Autism is our "religion." Some people have very dogmatic beliefs, and if you don't agree with them, you're damned, judged, and expelled.

You would think in a community where we are constantly fighting for acceptance and the rights of our children, we could all just get along and be more cohesive. I should feel safe to speak about my true feelings without being reprimanded or worried how my words are going to be taken. My feelings toward autism are just that— my feelings. I don't claim that they are the only way to feel, or even the right way to feel. They are solely mine, and I don't appreciate being coerced to the point where I feel I have to change my feelings in order to make someone else happy or fit into a belief system.

The autism community is divided on vaccinations, causes, cures, associations, doctors, treatments, home schooling, therapies, labels, inclusion, exclusion, services, awareness days, government funding, symbols and logos, accepting versus not accepting it, expectations, empathy versus sympathy versus pity, being a gift or not a gift, what to call it, and what is more politically correct to say—a person has autism or is a person autistic or on the spectrum?

Then there's that damn puzzle piece symbol! Why would people get so upset about a puzzle piece representing autism and being used as a universal symbol? I'm too bogged down in my own daily autism shit sandwich to care one way or another about a freaking puzzle piece. It could be a Lego, dinosaur, hot dog, black box, Scrabble tile or a question mark for all I care. But people are up in arms about it. They don't like being labeled as a puzzle piece or a mystery and some don't want anything to do with "lighting it up BLUE".

Sigh.

ETIQUETTE

Potty training is just one sensitive subject I wish people would stop trying to give me advice on, and the other big one is asking me how Dominic is doing with it.

"He's doing great," I excitedly reply. Then almost on cue, people ask the following question:

"Is he talking yet?"

"Uhm, no," I have to say, completely deflated.

Then I get "that" look. It's a look somewhere between a bolt of shock with wide eyes and deep pity with a sad face.

I think to myself, how in the hell do I get out of this? What do I say to this person feeling bad for me, but silently thanking God it's not them? Then, after the uncomfortable silence and if they aren't brain dead, they can sense my disappointment and frustration. That's when they assure me that any day now we are going to see a HUGE explosion of language and communication. They proceed to tell me that a friend of a friend's brother's nephew's cousin once removed didn't talk until he was seven. This is supposed to make me feel better or give me some kind of hope.

They keep talking, in a nervous almost uncontrollable chatter about how cute Dominic is and what beautiful eyes he has or how much he's grown. They'll reassuringly quip, "Oh, I'm sure he'll talk any day now, he's probably just going to be a late talker". And, that's when I smile politely and change the subject to the unbelievable price of gasoline or what's new with the Kardashians.

I know that most people mean well, but if I have to hear about one more cousin of a friend's distant daughter-in-law that someone knows with autism and how they were magically cured by some mixture of outer-space therapy while standing on their head eating coconut oil, I think I'll scream. Remember that just because you know who Temple Grandin is doesn't make you familiar with autism and the enormous spectrum that it is.

Some people must think that I just sit around with my head up my ass, that I haven't done any of my own research on the subject. Not to brag, but I've read over 45 books on the topic of autism and ways to cope and cure and understand and navigate the subject. I make the rounds on Google constantly researching Dominic's health, behavior, and other issues he and our entire family face. It is my life. I eat, breathe, sleep and crap autism.

While I appreciate the concern and excitement, unless you have a child with special needs and are going through firsthand what I am going through or actually are an expert, I don't want to hear the story of an autistic child in Alaska who can engineer a log cabin out of popsicle sticks or a kid in Mexico who can read sheet music and play the piano with his toes. Because, for every amazing and inspirational story out there about how a child is progressing with autism or has been "cured" of autism, there are a million stories of parents struggling with and seeing absolutely **no** progress at all from their child. My husband came up with a new term that means no progress – *progless. i.e.:* "We see a lot of *progless* around our house!"

I'm sorry if this seems harsh or cruel. Until this happened to us, I was one of those people who didn't know better. But you cannot imagine some of the insensitive things people have said to me without regard or a clue of how it will affect me. Would you tell a blind person about the beauty they are missing because they can't see? Or, would you tell a quadriplegic how you heard of a person who was once a quadriplegic and is now dancing across America and then send him or her the link to the awe-inspiring Youtube video?

So, please stop sending me links to what the media chooses to hype as hope for autism or autism awareness because those links to autism success stories do not motivate or inspire me. They're nice, just as a Hallmark card is nice. Don't get me wrong, I'm happy for the people whom those stories directly concern, but for me who is living in *Progless* Land, they are sad reminders of what's not to come or what may never be part of my son's story.

Temple Grandin's story was so astonishing that it was made into a mainstream movie starring Clair Danes. No doubt, Grandin is a genius— a doctor, engineer, inventor, animal activist, author, cowgirl, professor, motivational speaker, autism advocate, and much more. She's set the bar high for us with low-functioning kids with autism.

And, as wonderful and heartwarming as the story was of the boy with autism making a basket in the last minute of the high school game, it didn't give me any more hope for Dominic who might not make it to high school where he'll learn what a basketball is.

Newsflash! If these were everyday stories, they wouldn't make it to the news or go viral on the internet. They are only in the news because of their improbable likelihood. Furthermore, people only want to hear about the goodness in autism. No one wants to turn on the news and hear about parents of an autistic child who had to quit their job and lost their house to foreclosure in order to care for their severely autistic child, or how many parents of children with special needs are on antidepressants just to be able to get through the day. Making recent news, is the tragic story about the warrior-advocate mom who just couldn't take it anymore and tried to kill herself and her 14 year old overly aggressive daughter with autism with a lit bbq inside the family van. What makes a person snap? How much can one parent take? We all have limits.

Who wants to hear about the ugly and dark truth? Why isn't the news talking about issues of potty training children on the spectrum and the cost of adult diapers and why insurance companies will not cover them? Why doesn't the media talk about the severely affected autistic children and adults who bang their head against things and hurt themselves every day or become too aggressive and have to be institutionalized? Where is the truth about the dark side of autism and how much it sucks for the parents and household, as well as the children living it every day? Why doesn't the news do a story on the hardship having a child with special needs puts on a marriage? Or how it can divide a once tightly knit family?

Miracle cures are escapism, so I've considered making a YouTube channel dedicated to autism meltdowns so that people can see how it really is. Heartwarming? No! Newsworthy? No! Truthful? Yes! But who would ever watch it? Surely not parents with typical children, they couldn't relate. And, surely not parents (with an autistic child) who live the drama and nightmares every day.

So the only people who might tune in would be the morbidly curious or creepily fetish. The other purpose I could see this serving is for people who say stupid things to me, such as, "He'll grow out of it." Or, "He just needs a good spanking." And, my favorite, "You need to try this miracle treatment that I heard about in the UK," I can simply smile and hand them a card with my Meltdowns YouTube Channel and let them experience my autism reality in all its glory.

There. I have just offended almost everyone I know who has ever sent me a link to a heartwarming, uplifting story about autism. I'm sorry. I get it. I've read it. I've seen it. I've got the t-shirt. I've got my Google alert set to the subject. But not all things work for everyone. And when you try and try and try new things and they don't work, it's equivalent to banging your head and bank account against a brick wall. The failure and *progless* makes you feel worse than you originally thought you could feel.

The question I get asked most is, "Have you heard about that pretty blond Playboy actress, Jenny McCarthy, and how she "**cured**" her son by simply changing his diet?" Uhm, yes, I have. Unfortunately I have read all of her books from cover to cover back when I had high hopes. I had even put her name into my DVR wish list so that I could be alerted anytime she was coming on TV. I didn't want to miss any of her interviews. I am a card-toting member of *Generation Rescue,* and I have donated to several of their charity events. But, Jenny McCarthy's personal experience doesn't change Dominic's autism.

Autism is so complex because each case is different. Each individual child is different. Each circumstance is different. I wish people would stop lumping all autism cases into one defined circumstance with one distinct outcome. Something that worked miracles on a child in Germany, Ohio or for Jenny McCarthy's son may not work at all for your child or for my Dominic.

ASD MYTHS

Because autism is so misunderstood, I thought it might be helpful to debunk the top 11 myths about this curious disorder—

1. *Autistic people are all alike.*
    Not even close. The most common thing autistic people have in common is lack of communication and difficulty with social skills.
2. *All autistic people are geniuses or have amazing talents.*
    Not all people with autism are operating at genius or savant levels. In fact, most do not. You might even classify most people with "classic autism" as mentally retarded.
3. *Autistic people have poor communication skills, are nonverbal, and rock in a corner.*
    This would apply to those with a more severe or classic type of autism. Many people with autism can talk, do not rock in a corner, and can communicate with their words just fine.
4. *Autistic people were born "unloved" or by "refrigerator moms."*
    This was an old theory from the 1950s. Research has proven this to be 100% false.
5. *Autistic people don't feel love, empathy, or compassion.*

While emotions and social skills are a challenge for a high percentage of people with autism, many can feel and exhibit a range of emotions, including love, compassion, empathy, and sympathy.

6. *Vaccinations cause autism.*

The Wakefield Theory has been discredited that vaccinations cause autism. I think the jury is still out on this one. It would make more sense to say that vaccinations may contribute to health and neurological issues in children who are sensitive to the injections or who may have other medical issues going on.

7. *Autism is a mental health disorder.*

It's a neurological condition, much different than a mental illness or mental disorder. An autistic person, however, can be affected by both autism and a mental illness.

8. *Autistic people are hiding behind their diagnosis, using it as an excuse.*

Who would want to be diagnosed with autism and all of its challenges if given the choice? Some autistic people have learning difficulties and developmental delays – all a subset of the symptoms on the autism spectrum.

9. *Autistic people are a danger to themselves and/or society.*

Even though some autistic people are prone to hurting themselves or lashing out against others by hitting, biting, banging their heads against something when they get agitated, it's not the norm.

10. *Autism can be cured.*

While there are many therapies that can help a person with autism overcome their symptoms and issues and function at a higher level, I have yet to see any person (including Jenny McCarthy's son) completely cured of autism and all it brings.

11. Autistic people cannot live productive, independent lives.
Many people on the autism spectrum are leading brilliant, productive, independent lives, depending on the level of severity of the autism and where they fall on the autism spectrum. Most people with classic or severe autism cannot lead independent lives as an adult and need to be monitored and cared for.

Most of the above list of myths is based on stereotyping. Autism looks different to everyone. For Dominic, it's a combination of developmental delays, no talking, lots of screaming, severe medical issues, short-term memory loss and losing things, impulsiveness with no sense of danger, wandering, insomnia, impatience, frequent meltdowns, social challenges, and acute OCD and ADHD.

SHRINKING OPTIONS

When you have a child with special needs, things change. Your options change. Things you may have taken for granted at one time, the little things— sleep, taking a shower, finishing a cup of coffee while it's still hot, leaving the house, leaving the house on time, spontaneity of any kind, vacations, daytime trips to the grocery store, stopping at a red light, pumping gas, riding an elevator in peace, happiness, an enjoyable and relaxed sex life— those are things that become a fantasy, something you long for like a far-distant dream, one of those maybe someday dreams.

When you have a child with special needs, your options shrink based on the severity of your child's disability. Sit-down dinners in nice restaurants are no longer an option; you must get things "to go." It becomes which fast food restaurant has the shortest line in the drive-through coupled with what your picky autistic eater will eat!

What? Did I just call autism a disability? Yes, I did. Why? Because for many it is. So are uncontrolled seizures and any other special needs side dishes you get served with a main dish of autism.

To clarify my definition, I am not lumping all autism into one category. There are very different levels of autism and symptoms of autism. I am not labeling all people with autism as disabled. I know there are many, many people on the spectrum that are the complete opposite of disabled. I am not referring to the capable, independent, verbal, Einstein and genius people who can function on their own with minimal care or without any care at all. So, if you disagree with me, that my son's autism is not a form of a genuine disability, I invite you to come and live at my house for just one day!

Imagine trying to find a place in a public restroom to surreptitiously change your seven-year-old's diapers. I've seen the looks, stares, and elbow nudges people give each other when I enter a woman's restroom with my giant, 7 year old son. I'm not sure what the hubbub is all about. He's surely not checking you out in there! He is completely unaware of you. Believe me, I'm just as uncomfortable trying to go unnoticed, but that's hard to do when he's screaming. I'm just trying to make it out of the restroom alive with a tiny bit of dignity before he touches something gross.

Options are diminishing as I type this— things like where can you warm a baby bottle for your seven year old, trying to find baby sitters who aren't too freaked out by bad behavior to watch him and be able to handle his medically fragile issues. I need to find a nurse with strong bladder control because in the 3-4 minutes it might take a nurse to use the restroom, Dominic can swiftly be out the door and down the street. Nurses happen to be a little more expensive than your 15-year-old teenage neighbor looking to make an easy $10 per hour to watch your child. Going somewhere with your 4 ½ ft. - 65-pound special needs child who no longer fits into a stroller or a shopping cart is next to impossible. Certainly, you can't carry him around. It's time to trade the stroller in for a wheelchair.

Options for your child's future have dwindled to almost nothing when you have a nonverbal child with impulsive and wandering tendencies, epilepsy, poor balance and motor coordination, and who is not potty trained. When I take Dominic somewhere public, I cannot let go of his hand for one second. It takes one second for him to take off and become a huge danger to himself on an escalator or in a parking lot. He has no sense of fear or consequences so I must hold on tight to him always.

You will, however, pick up some amazing skills along the way. These aren't things you can necessarily put on a resume but you'll become very resourceful. You'll become an expert research analyst, and you will gain an excellent aptitude for debating with people who think they know more than you about a subject you live and breathe on a daily basis.

Learning that your child has a developmental disorder is hard. These are the questions that keep rattling around in my head every day—

Was it in our genes? Hereditary and we just didn't know? Did it skip a generation? Was it something I ate during my pregnancy? I steered clear of deli meats and soft cheeses. Did I not eat enough fruits and vegetables? Was it the pesticides on the fruits and vegetables that I did eat? Was it the numerous immunizations? Was it food allergies? How about the work I had done at the dentist, removing my mercury fillings while I was breastfeeding? High metal toxicity? A virus, mine or his? Lyme disease? Old eggs? Bad sperm? A combination? Was it toxic cleaning supplies? A brain malformation? Was it the chemical BPA toxins in his plastic baby bottles? Or, all the bottled water I was drinking in order to be "healthy"? Lack of folic acid or a vitamin deficiency? Was it the new construction toxins in the paint, sheetrock, carpet glue? Pesticide from the vineyard? Luck of the draw? Bad Karma? Payback? When will I stop asking these questions? Where's my keys? Why is this so hard?

Why was I so selfish to want another child at the age of almost 40? What did I expect? Why couldn't I leave well enough alone and be happy with what I had? I was happily married, had a great job as a realtor in a booming market, and had a beautiful neuro-typical son. My husband and I were getting ready to build our dream home. Why did I always have to want more? Was it all because I wanted a sibling for my older son? Sometimes I wish I had a do-over, so that I could go back and fix what went wrong, whatever "it" was.

THREE

THE SYSTEM

THE GREAT DIVIDE

P rior to going to Stanford, I had taken Dominic to a specialist DAN! doctor (Defeat Autism Now!). They have a holistic approach to treating autism. Most of them believe that vaccinations play a role in autism, along with issues like Lyme Disease, heavy metal toxicity, Candida overload, vitamin deficiencies, etc. DAN! doctors also have different ideas of treating autism biomedically i.e., oxygen therapies, antibiotic therapies, vitamin shots, detoxification, diet, etc. Celebrity and autism advocate, Jenny McCarthy, took her son to a DAN! doctor and supposedly had amazing results. She claims he was "cured." What kind of mom would I be if I didn't at least check into every therapy possible?

So I did.

Unfortunately, we had a devastatingly negative experience with an unethical DAN! doctor/neurologist/massage therapist/aura reader with a proclivity for lying in San Rafael, California. Later I found out that this "doctor" had a habit of taking advantage of patients and their families during very difficult times. I know this because since blogging about our experience with this "doctor", I have been contacted by numerous other victims of her unethical practices. I have complained to the Medical Board and anywhere else I can think of to document our experience with her.

When allopathic doctors find out that we've tried an alternative path, we are told in no uncertain terms that we've been foolish or careless in seeking this kind of treatment.

With alternative biomedical theories out there in the media, one would have to live in a cave to not have heard about them if you have a child with autism. I'm not in the holistic or allopathic camp. I just want to try everything and not dismiss anything. As I've said many times, I have no freaking idea what caused these conditions in Dominic. If some of the remedies don't work, it's not as though I'm out anything, other than a great deal of money. But, I couldn't live with myself if I knew something existed out there that might help Dominic, and I didn't try it.

I'm not saying that the DAN! doctors have all the answers or even a "cure." I'm just saying that they seem to be the only doctors trying new things and interested in finding a cure. They are more than willing to work with parents. They're usually more patient than allopathic doctors, although they also charge upwards of $500 per hour and most don't accept insurance, not to worry because most insurance companies don't cover alternative practices anyway. If a DAN! doctor could give us positive results and help Dominic speak, cope, and become more independent, it would be worth the $500 per hour fee. I would take a graveyard-shift job and sell a kidney to pay the bills! It's that important to me.

Dominic has a massive amount of medical challenges on top of the developmental and behavioral issues. I'm pretty convinced they are all connected somehow. What I don't know and can't get answers to is whether the autism is causing the medical issues or the medical issues are causing the autism and developmental delays. The doctors just don't know. Which came first...the chicken or the egg?

Dominic is defined as medically fragile. He has a laundry list of symptoms and conditions too long to list. You would not believe the diagnoses that have come up by typing Dominic's medical issues into WebMD. I'm at a crossroads, not sure what to believe anymore. All the tests keep coming back "normal." Yet, how can a child having 80+ seizures a day be "normal"? My online bachelor's degree in Epilepsy 101 has left me dumbfounded as to what is real and what to believe.

Dominic was a huge pain in the ass and completely out of control at our last neurology checkup at UCSF, although nothing out of the ordinary for us. He was just his normal self— screaming, kicking, taking off his shoes and throwing them at the nurse. The doctor was appalled and asked me if I was giving him anything for his behavior. I replied that I had actually never considered it. In one swoop I was handed a prescription for Resperidol. She said it would "calm" him. I wearily took the prescription and considered giving it to him in case it might help.

I even had the prescription filled, but when it came down to it, I could not do it. For me, behavior medications need to be a complete last resort. I need to keep something in my arsenal for the future autism I face, for the aggressive teenage years when he is taller and stronger than I am. Maybe I would feel differently about this if he weren't already taking the daily maximum amount of anti-seizure medications, Depakote and Keppra. And maybe I would feel differently about them if he didn't have epilepsy and a weak liver.

DOCTORS

Sadly, I'm still struggling to find the right option for medical care for Dominic. As mentioned, we've had three pediatricians, two neurologists, and one disgraceful DAN! doctor. When Dominic gets sick, I have to take him to the emergency room because I won't stand for an arrogant, dismissive doctor with no compassion and a poor bedside manner. In my situation, I need all of the support I can get and so far, it has never come in the form of a Pediatrician.

Our first pediatrician literally told me I was crazy for thinking Dominic was autistic at 13 months old. I was told they do not diagnose autism until around 3 years old. He laughed me out of the exam room and said, "In my heart of hearts, Dominic does not have autism." I had just watched Jenny McCarthy appear on Oprah talking about her son having autism and how she "cured" him. Everything she described about her son and his mannerisms and stimming (repetitive motions) was spot on for Dominic.

As a baby, we thought Dominic was just quirky. Even as a newborn he had some curious traits. I used to think it was so cute the way he would wave to the sky. We used to joke that maybe he saw dead people. We thought he was going to have such strong calf muscles from standing on his toes. How talented he was that he loved to open and close doors at such a young age. We made jokes about how Dominic was going to be a doorman when he grew up. How funny, we thought, that he would flap his arms when he got excited and how he would lay on his stomach and kick his foot up and down or scratch the walls with his fingernails. It was the not talking or walking at 15 months that alarmed us.

Autism did not run in our family. So, how did we know he was autistic when I had zero experience with autism and had never been around it? I chalk it up to motherly instinct and an episode of Oprah. I knew something was wrong.

At 13 months old, Dominic had not hit many of his milestones, including the two main ones: walking and talking. Although he seemed mentally engaged, he crawled everywhere and never attempted to speak. He seemed to have the strength in his legs because he could stand and would sometimes walk around furniture holding onto or pushing a cart, but he would not walk on his own. When he did walk, he toe-walked. He also did not make any sounds, purposely or otherwise. He cried (a lot) and grunted and that was it. He didn't babble or speak any form of baby talk. He couldn't imitate or follow simple commands, such as "Touch your nose." or "Point to the cat." or "Where's Dominic?" He had weird sensory issues. He gagged a lot, couldn't chew his food properly, stuffed his mouth with food as if he couldn't tell when it was full and then he would choke. His coordination was poor, and his gait was off.

He had terrible sleep patterns, even as an infant, because he was an insomniac. He never slept more than a few hours at a time, and still doesn't. His dexterity was delayed, and he couldn't do a pincher grasp, nor would he point to things. And, the biggest red flag for me was his terrible mood swings. He was either happy or miserable. There was nothing much in between. His mood swings would go from zero to sixty with no warning. Looking back, he was almost manic, exhibiting OCD and ADHD traits.

After Dominic consistently complained daily of head pain by pointing to his head and screaming daily for at least a year, I asked the neurologist at UCSF if he could do another MRI to make sure it wasn't something like a tumor or cyst. I was told, "No, you don't just get to randomly request an MRI." I got irritated, pissed off actually, and told them they better hope it was nothing serious or there would be legal consequences. After that threat, they finally agreed and Dominic had another MRI last summer.

The MRI came back with some surprising results. The good news was that he did not have a brain tumor. But, besides the main course of epilepsy with a side order of autism, it was revealed that Dominic has an issue with his brain being under-developed. Dominic apparently has the following issues with his brain: thinning of the corpus callosum, cerebellar dysgenesis and mega cisterna magna. More big words to add to my medical vocabulary list!

Supposedly, according to his neurologist, it is not "progressive," meaning "it" will stay at this level of underdevelopment and not get any worse. What does this mean? Does it mean he will never further develop? Does this explain why he is stuck cognitively at about age 12-14 months?

What is maddening is the results from his last MRI in 2009 which said everything was "normal." I questioned it then. I kept asking the doctors how he could have "normal" MRIs, EEGs and CTs and be this medically and developmentally challenged. So, I asked our neurologist if he would compare the 2009 MRI to the 2012 MRI to see if this issue was there in 2009 and how it got overlooked. It wasn't until months later that I received the news back that it was not "progressive."

I still don't know what exactly this last batch of findings with Dominic's brain means. The doctor has not taken any time to explain it to me other than a brief paragraph in an email. When do you say enough is enough when dealing with doctors and demand the courtesy of some kind of explanation?

Do they want to see him again for more testing? Nope. What does this mean for his future? Do they tell me how this may be affecting his development or if it is the cause of his seizures, headaches, or autism? Nope. Nothing. I am left to my own sleepless imagination and unanswered questions; which is a dangerous thing when you combine it with copious amounts of chocolate, Google searches, and WebMD.

What I have learned from the medical community, in general, and I can only speak from my own experience, is that doctors do not want to deal with kids with special needs, especially autism. They don't have the extra time it takes or the patience. I know Dominic is not an easy patient. Epilepsy just happens to be one of those specialty fields where no one really knows that much about it. They really don't know that much about autism and epilepsy or how or why they are connected. There are so many theories out there and no doctor wants to be wrong. So, the medical profession just puts a band-aid on it in the form of a prescription and moves on to the next patient.

I have a neuro-typical child who has gone to the same doctors as my special needs child. Fact is, they get treated differently. I get treated differently depending which kid I'm with. When I have an appointment for Dominic, the bedside manner is seriously lacking. Most of the time the doctor has one hand on the door handle of the exam room trying to get out of the appointment as quickly as possible because he knows the questions are coming or they have a 1 p.m. tee time.

One thing I have learned is that no doctor likes to admit that he or she has no answer when you ask a question. And when you ask as many questions as I do, that's when the doctor begins to shut down, ignore, and avoid you. I'm sure I've been labeled as one of those difficult or combative mothers. Suddenly, when you make appointments, you are now seeing a nurse practitioner. I imagine Dominic's chart says that his mother is obsessed with WebMD.

When my first son Jimmy was born, we were given the name of a wonderful and experienced pediatrician in our city. He was the best! We saw him for 10 years with absolutely no complaints. It wasn't until Dominic was born and I made an appointment with this Doctor to tell him my concerns about his developmental delays and other issues that I thought was related to autism that I realized he was not a good match for Dominic.

He was appalled that I had formed my opinion based on watching Jenny McCarthy on Oprah. He laughed me out the office, literally rolling his eyes at me and telling me not to get my medical advice from a bikini model and to stay away from WebMD. Fortunately, I was tenacious and insisted on a second opinion, and that was when I found out that Dominic was indeed on the autism spectrum.

Do you think I ever got an apology or heard an ooops, you were right from this Pediatrician? Instead, when I had to bring Dominic to his office for subsequent visits—I never got to see the actual Doctor. I would see another Doctor in the practice or a Nurse Practitioner. Obviously, I felt like he may be avoiding me since I could see his car in the parking lot. Then I had to second guess my sanity and wonder if it was just me…was I being paranoid and overly sensitive?

The final straw with this Pediatrician was when Dominic was hospitalized during the weekend from hell due to a multitude of grand mal seizures. We had been in the hospital for two days and our Pediatrician who was on the floor and happened to be the on call Pediatrician never made an appearance even though he knew we were there. He was doing rounds on the floor, I heard his voice in the room next door and I assumed he would be stopping by our room next. He never did. When I asked the nurse when he would be coming in, she said, "Oh, I thought he did come in and see you"? Nope. He did not. She told me he must have "forgotten" or gotten "busy".

It's hard finding good, compassionate care when you have an autistic child. Another instance was when Dominic was 4 years old he broke his shin bone and when we went into the Orthopedic Doctor's office to have the cast removed, Dominic was screaming and crying (nothing out of the ordinary). The doctor said, "If you don't get him to shut up and stop crying, I will have to ask you to leave". He refused to touch Dominic and made me take off the cast myself. Yes, I was still charged $150 for that office visit even though I did all the work.

I've decided that I must watch too many episodes of *Grey's Anatomy* because my expectations of doctors seem very unrealistic. I grew up watching *Marcus Welby, MD* and I was under some delusional impression that doctors became doctors because they really cared about helping people. Maybe I'm naïve and jaded, but I have not met a doctor in the last decade that really seems to care. It's all about the money. Rush-rush, one hand on the door, don't have much time to talk. They want to keep the questions to a minimum, and their recurring tone is mostly, "Deal with it lady."

This goes for the nurses, too. During that hospital stay at Stanford, I had to summon a nurse to relieve me for 5 minutes so that I could go pee. I had held my urine so much during that stay that I had gotten a bladder infection! Every time I hit the nurse button, I felt like I was bothering someone. Nobody ever asked me if I needed anything. No one asked if I would like a break to go get dinner or a cup of coffee. Even when I had barf all over me one morning, I couldn't go into the bathroom and get out of my clothes.

I've never been afraid of confrontation. But, the stress of Dominic has made me even more vocal. I'm not taking crap from these people who are getting paid a lot of money to do their jobs, which should include having a smidgen of kindness and empathy for what the patient and the family are going through.

IN HOME NURSES

I work full time from home. In order to be able to get anything done, we have nurses who come to the house to care for Dominic. It's not an easy job to take care of him. He's not always cooperative, and he tantrums a lot. It's hard watching someone else's child, especially when they are nonverbal, autistic, and have behavioral issues. I know he's hard, but what's harder is having someone in your house taking care of your child and hearing the turmoil that goes on from both sides—the nurse's and Dominic's.

Right now we have a couple of nurses who are amazing, but it hasn't always been like that. We've had nurses come and go. And when you open up your home to someone and let them into your family, it goes without saying that you have certain expectations.

We had a nurse when Dominic was three years old and in the thick of the seizures. This nurse didn't have children of her own and didn't come equipped with the patience or compassion required to care for a Dominic. It was clear she was hoping for an easy child who would sit in bed and sleep. Dominic had so much energy that he bounced off the walls. He was so jacked up on anti-seizure medications that few moments were left to sit and relax and read a book unless he was cat-napping.

You could tell she didn't want to be with Dominic. She wasn't very nice to him and pretty much just verbally badgered him all day. If he hurt himself, got frustrated or cried, she made no attempt to soothe him. I didn't like her tone or the way she talked down to him. She was condescending and always yelling at him.

One day I was upstairs in the office working and I could hear her: *"Stop it. Don't do that. No. No. No. I said No. Don't touch it. Get out of there. Sit down. All right that's it. Well, you shouldn't have taken off your shoes. No. I said No."*

All I could think of was if she treated him like this when I was home and she knew I could hear her, how was she treating him when I left the house? I considered getting a nanny-cam. I know more than anyone that Dominic is a very challenging, spirited child most of the time. His screams all start and end the same. You can't tell if something is truly wrong like a fork in the eye or if the DVD he is watching froze. That is why it takes a special kind of person to be able to care for him and want to help calm and soothe him.

I could hear the nurse yelling at Dominic to finish his yogurt. And then he took off his shoes. Dominic was crying, and she began one of her rants. I walked into the room where they were, picked him up and gave him a hug. He couldn't have been happier to see me.

I asked her point blank if she knew he was autistic. She stuttered a bit, a little taken aback by my direct question. So I stared at her square in the eyes and waited for her reply. She said, "Yes, I know." So I asked her if she had ever taken care of an autistic child before. And she said, "No, but my friend has one of *them*. She continued to jam her foot into her mouth when she told me her friend does have some help for "*it.*"

I became a mama bear and went off on one of my tirades and explained to her how Dominic doesn't understand half of what she is saying to him because she's talking too fast, that it all sounds like yelling and that he needs to be treated with some kindness. He doesn't respond well to constant yelling.

She tried to argue with me that she wasn't yelling at him but just giving him clear directions loudly. WTF? I said, "For one, I'm right here. You're yelling at him and number two, he's autistic, not deaf."

I told her that trying to teach him a lesson by not letting him go outside because he took his shoes off was futile, that she couldn't sit and try to have a battle of wits with him and verbally beat him down to a point where he would understand her thinking. I told her that he spends a good deal of the time with her upset and crying, that it was hard for me to listen to her treat him that way, and that if she lets him get too upset she was going to throw him into a seizure.

I told her it was probably a good idea that she leave because her presence was making me crazy. I called the agency and told them not to send her to our house ever again, that I'd rather have no help than to have her help. When I first called the agency, I felt as though I was tattling on someone and I felt guilty, but then I realized, wait a minute, my son cannot speak or speak up. I am Dominic's voice and advocate. If I don't stand up for him, who in this lifetime will? That was a defining, ah-ha moment for me.

SLEEP STUDY — EEG

After a series of many grand mal seizures and with no luck controlling them with medication, we were referred to Stanford Medical Center for an overnight sleep study from our Santa Rosa Neurologist. Even though Dominic had already had numerous EEG's, they weren't catching any of the head drops or grand mals because they were short, brief studies. Unless Dominic happened to have a seizure while the EEG was hooked to his head, they couldn't get much information. The EEG's kept coming back "normal."

At this time in his life Dominic had an obsession with shopping carts. I brought Dominic's cart so that he could have an ounce of pleasure during his long EEG sleep study. I must be either stupid or I wasn't paying very close attention when they explained EEG procedure to me. I was told Dominic would be able to walk around the room and be mobile. I just assumed in this day and age of technology, satellites, and wireless communication that when they told me he would be able to walk around, it would not mean a two year old would have to carry a seven pound power-pack and drag a twelve-foot industrial extension cord around with him. He could have walked around if he had super powers maybe. He could have walked around if he wasn't dragging a large computer screen and cart with a hard drive attached to his head via long and heavy electrical cords, like the industrial kind you'd find in your garage.

I had to shadow his every move and follow next to him holding his power pack, hoping he wasn't going to trip on the extension cord or slam to the ground from a seizure. Where was the hospital's safety manual? He kept grabbing the cords, which, did I mention, were attached to his head? And all I could think about is where had that long filthy cord been? Where in the hospital had this cord been dragged across a dirty, germ-filled floor and now my baby was handling it and then nonchalantly putting his hands in his mouth. I had never had germaphobe tendencies until that day at Stanford. The nurse rolled her eyes when I asked her for some disinfectant wipes so that I could clean the cord.

I'm sure I was labeled "difficult." Oh well.

After we arrived, first order of business was for the EEG tech to hook Dominic up, and not in a good way. She began by swabbing something on Dominic's head, which was a highly toxic glue resembling and smelling like industrial Rubber Cement. I was really confused because the glue was not the same kind of glue we were used to at our local hometown hospital. When the technician first cracked open the glue, I could immediately smell it. The chemical smell was stronger than anything I had ever smelled before. Then I watched her begin to put it into Dominic's hair and onto his scalp…

"Oh no, please stop," I said. I got pretty upset and I asked her what she was doing. She responded with a shrug and told me it was the glue for the EEG leads.

"It's not ventilated in here. Can you open a window? If I'm getting a headache from the fumes, you are not putting that on my baby's scalp. What is it?" I asked.

She assured me it was safe, but from the odor, I could tell there was no way this could be safe. Then she told me not to worry; acetone easily dissolves it! I told her we would be checking out and foregoing this procedure if that was the only way to do this. I asked the obvious question, "Why in Santa Rosa did they use a safe, nontoxic blue gel and a cute little cap to hold the leads on? Again I got the shrug. She waited a few minutes, I guess to think of an answer and responded with, "The caps don't work because the head sizes vary so much."

"Uh, Huh, that is why they make the caps in different sizes, for the different sized heads…small, medium, large." I retorted.

She stared at me again, holding the container of liquid cement, which actually had a skull and crossbones on the warning label. The technician left the room to check with a supervisor. When she returned, she told me that she didn't have to use the glue; she could use special tape. Really? What a swell idea! I thanked her, and then she wrapped Dominic's head in gauze and a purple turban while he screamed.

I thought the sleep study was going to be super high tech but was surprised again that if and when Dominic did move and drag the cord and power pack around the room, I had to manually move the camera to follow him. Controlling the camera was virtually impossible because it was my other full-time job to hold the power pack and make sure he didn't trip on the cords. I was now Mom/Safety Director/Videographer who seriously needed to pee.

My mom came down to visit and brought Dominic a backpack. Now if he wanted to walk around the room, we could stick the giant power pack in the backpack, freeing up one of my hands to carry the cord and operate the camera.

The day before our Stanford trip, Dominic had at least 20 seizures. When we arrived at Stanford, Dominic hadn't had one yet. He was seizure-free. Was it stage fright? I had never wanted him to have a seizure before, but now we needed him to or the visit would be an expensive waste of time.

Be careful of what you wish for…

I watched him have around 30. Each time he had a seizure, I had been directed to push a little button and I did. He woke up bright eyed and bushy tailed at 4:00 a.m., and he wanted to watch cartoons. Since it looked like high noon in our room because of all the lights on in the hallway, I could not get him to go back to sleep. The nurse made him a bottle and then 30 minutes later, he projectile vomited all over himself and me. We had to cut his pajamas off of him because we couldn't get them over his hardwired turban wrapped head. The bandage holding the EEG leads on his head had come off twice during the night, and only a little point on the top of his head remained.

Dominic had numerous head-drop seizures, and I kept track and pushed the little button each time they occurred. Thankfully, by noon the doctor had seen enough of the seizures on the EEG video recording and told me we could go home. We thought we were going to have to be there for 2 or 3 days/nights, but the good news/bad news was that in the first 24 hours they had received enough seizure activity data, approximately 100 seizures. They had more than they needed.

Some of Dominic's seizures are called "absence seizures" and again, being brand new to epilepsy, I had never heard of such a thing. I was shown in the video when the EEG registered an "absence seizure." You would never have known it was a seizure. Dominic looked still and content, wide-awake, and quietly watching his cartoon. It makes me wonder how many of those he has per day now and I just don't know it.

I did get some answers. The seizures are generalized and the hardest kind to control. The Stanford doctor told us Dominic has a severe form of epilepsy and would have it for the rest of his life. He suggested I get him a better helmet, patted me on the back and gave me another new prescription for Dominic to try. He also ordered some genetic blood tests.

Sigh.

SPECIAL EDUCATION

Typical school or home school an autistic child? That is a hot topic in my world. But what do I know about early childhood development? Nothing. Am I an expert in this field? No. Do I think I could do a good job? Not really. In our case, I'm choosing to leave Dominic's education up to the professionals. And, since, social skills and lack-there-of are a huge obstacle with children on the spectrum, why would I want to take him out of a social environment? I want him to be social and socialized with other children. I want him to try his best to navigate and develop teacher-student relationships. I want him to be excited to go to school and ride the short bus and to learn things in a variety of ways that I could never teach him. I want him to have experiences that I could never give him if he just stayed home with me.

I'll be honest. I'm already spent. I do not think I could handle 24/7 with Dominic in a parenting role and teaching role, especially trying to teach him things over and over and over. I love him to pieces, but at some point I would hit a wall and my teaching and parenting skills would collide and suffer. I already feel a huge responsibility to help him any way that I can as his mom. I cannot fathom bearing the burden of his learning and educational development.

I'm choosing special education, and although those words are tough words to utter, I am grateful that he has the opportunity to go to a school classroom and learn what he can from the professionals. The teachers, aids, and therapists have to be bordering on sainthood to devote their lives and careers to teaching our special needs children. It can't be easy, and we all know the pay is not great.

The Individual Education Plan (IEP) meetings are tough for me. Like most parents, I spend hours and hours before the meeting pouring over the last set of goals and rewriting them, taking notes and making a case for justifying any services or therapies I feel are needed that will help Dominic short term and long term.

I do my very best not to cry at the IEP meeting, but I can't help it when they play a five-minute slide show of Dominic throughout the school year in slow motion with special effects to a sad song soundtrack and captions as if Dominic is speaking. Imagine someone taking your biggest heartbreak in life and putting it in slow motion to Louie Armstrong singing, "What a Wonderful World"? It gets me every time, and I'm not sure if it's a gesture of kindness or if the intention is to unarm the already fired-up parents in a moment of weakness. I can't help but wonder if studies have been done proving that parents who get emotional and cry during the slideshow portion of the meeting actually ask less of the school district in the way of services. I assume I can't be the only parent breaking down at the table since they have strategically placed Kleenex boxes near me. I can't wait for the IEP meeting when I am finally unfazed by my sadness and forget to sob.

Once seated around the little kids table in tiny, little, uncomfortable chairs, knees hitting your chin in the medically fragile special needs classroom, your meeting is almost ready to begin. Our IEPs usually don't begin punctually, which leaves ample time to gaze at the pictures of the severely disabled classmates of your child, wheelchairs, and handicap devices staring you down. I had a moment of "Wow, this is really happening, I have a severely **disabled** child." Then the guilt creeps in and I remember to pull up my "big girl panties" because things could be worse.

I know that the teachers, aids, therapists, principals, etc. have done this process hundreds, possibly thousands of times, but listening to these people talk about my son in such clinical terms with little or no emotion becomes too much for me, and I have to go to my happy place when the lump in my throat starts cutting off my air. It's devastating, even though I know its true how very, very challenged and developmentally delayed my son truly is. To sit and talk about his learning delays, his physical disabilities, his medical challenges, and behavioral issues is excruciating because there is no running and hiding or burying my head in the sand like I can manage to do at home.

It's an eye-opening experience, knowing that things have gotten progressively worse in most areas. I'm wondering how unrealistic my expectations are for him. Each end-of-the-year report has the same theme. Each report starts out with what a delight he is and then moves on to talk about his bad behaviors, tantrums, screaming, hitting, throwing, and running away. He sounds like such a monster and the mama bear in me gets defensive until I put the proverbial pause button on, take a deep breath, and remember that the system is actually validating my daily issues with Dominic.

They go over Dominic's goals from the school year, and usually, we end up keeping most of them for the next year. That's how little progress is being made. Out of 10 basic goals, Dominic is lucky to hit 3 of them. I love how they describe his success or lack of success in terms of clinical trials, i.e, 4 out of 10 times he will do "such and such" as if he's a lab-rat. It's extremely frustrating knowing that your child isn't making much improvement at all. Some goals get purposely left off for the following year. I could make a case that they were giving up. At our last IEP, they said Dominic's name 194 times. All I could think about was how hammered I would have been if we were playing a drinking game and "Dominic" was the word you had to do a shot to every time someone said his name.

My mood, sleep deficit and current level of resilience determine how much I can tolerate at an IEP. I do my best to get a good night's sleep the night before. If I feel like they are really not concerned with what is best for Dominic and purposely trying to get out of something, I sometimes snap, like the time we went around and around on whether sucking and blowing belonged as a goal with the occupational therapist or the speech therapist and then magically ended up disappearing off the goals list entirely. Both made an argument that it was the other's role and shrugged the responsibility, which made it that neither one did anything for Dominic.

Most of the time I go through my day as though it's just a bad dream, and I'm going to wake up any minute and everything is going to be okay. Like he's going to talk. Like he's going to catch up. Like he's going to fit in. Like he's going to be normal. If I could only will him a better and easier quality of life, I would.

What about mainstreaming? As a child with special needs, Dominic has the right to an individual education plan in the "least restrictive" environment. The goal and the message for "our" kids is to mainstream them with the general population (*aka: the normal kids*). Yet, it seems to me the system goes out of its way to do things that would make the "special" kid stand out even more and, perhaps, feel more alienated. Making them ride on short buses, sticking them out in trailers on the back side of the school grounds away from the other classrooms, and giving them different recess and lunch times away from the other students. Where is the integration? I'm left scratching my head on this one.

How is this mainstreaming my child? And whoever said I wanted my child mainstreamed? The Office of Education was the one that gave me a hard time when I told them I wanted to put Dominic into a private school for autistic children only. I was told over and over what a bad idea that was because he would be missing out and not in "the least restrictive environment." My only point is— stop telling me that is what you are doing and then do something completely different. They aren't mainstreaming Dominic just because they let him attend an all classroom school assembly or special function once a year.

I arrived at Dominic's new special **education class,** and the first thing I noticed was that they had a big sign on the door that said "SPECIAL EDUCATION." This wasn't a handwritten sign for open house night for the parents who might have a hard time finding the room out on the back 40 of the school grounds. It is a permanent sign on the classroom alerting everyone that this is definitely the special ed classroom for the special kids in case there was ever any confusion. You wouldn't want to mix up the normals with the specials thinking they're in a classroom all together! As if I didn't know before I entered the classroom that I have a special boy in a special classroom. Thank goodness for that special sign on the door! It makes me wonder how the children in special ed classes that are able to read feel about the labeling on the classroom door.

Oh how I used to love summer, warm, sunny days and daylight savings which meant, longer days. Now summer means no school and more hours in the day for an autistic child to be thrown off from his normal routine. More hours in the day for Dominic to be bored and tantrum. More hours in the day to not sleep. More hours in the day to break things. More hours in the day to regress.

When summer officially starts at our house, it isn't long before I'm finding new things to lock up or hide while keeping Dominic out of the refrigerator, off the counters, out of the pantry, from throwing things in the toilet and from scaling the cabinet to get to the DVDs. To say he is a little OCD about things is a complete understatement! Summertime seems to magnify his OCD. Keeping him away from sharp objects and contained in the house for long periods of time can be a challenge. Going to the park and the beach are options, but with all of the kids out of school, crowds are not ideal for us either. At the end of every summer, my husband and I are eager to get Dominic ready for the short bus

THE SHORT BUS

The short bus has arrived! It's a joke and stigma in the "neuro-typical" world. I've heard the short bus jokes. And even though it's been making an appearance at our house now for 3 years, I still haven't gotten used to the beep, beep, beeping of the short bus backing up down our driveway. It's a personal issue I have and I can't help but want to sob each day it makes a grand arrival at our house. As much as I love the bus drivers, they're never on time. I know how hard it is getting Dominic ready and on the bus each day, so I can only imagine the delays with some of the other "special kids". It's just especially hard because Dominic has no patience or concept of time. He can't physically wait for something without melting down. He can't tell the difference between waiting 2 minutes or 20 minutes.

The days the bus is on time will most certainly be the days Dominic decides to undress himself or poop in his pants as the bus is backing up. I'm frantically trying to get him ready as fast as possible so that the bus doesn't have to wait, but if we're running at all late and not out the door, the bus driver backs up again and again so that I can hear the taunting of the beep…beeeeep…beeeeep of the bus. It's loud and sharp, making its point to me over and over, reminding me with every single beep that my kid rides the short bus! "I get it!!!" I want to scream. The bus driver uses the back up beeping even when they aren't backing up…she uses it as a tool to rouse me as if it's an alarm clock and I'm not going fast enough.

Sometimes by the time I get out the door, I'm already frazzled from the CBS Survivor-like challenge I just mastered getting Dominic ready. Some days it's too much for me to even watch the short bus drive away with Dominic on it. I look the other way, not making it back inside without a full, five-alarm ugly-cry breakdown. Some days I feel strong, hopeful and resilient; other days I question my better judgment in bringing kids into this world.

I could just drive him, but my whiney excuse why I don't want to drive him is worse and hurts to even say out loud. It's still too painful. I can barely stand to go into Dominic's classroom because it fully breaks what is left of my heart. The classroom is amazing; the people and kids are great; but there are so many kids with varying degrees of special needs and medical issues that it's hard for me to be around without getting very emotional. I fight back the tears. I don't want to be known as the cry baby or crazy mom so I just stay away.

There is a little boy with Down Syndrome in the class that is the sweetest, cutest, nicest, warmest, most loving child. Without fail he approaches me for a hug. I want to squeeze him. Every time I see him he asks me if I'm Dominic's mom and I always tell him yes. Then he tells me his name. It's very endearing, and I can't help but be envious that he can talk and Dominic can't. His mom gets to hear his sweet talking voice, not just his screaming voice and shrieks. His mom gets to hear him say, "I love you." I've actually had people say things to me like "Aren't you glad Dominic doesn't have Down's?" And, as completely inappropriate as that question is, no, I'm really not.

Dominic is all the way to the right on the special spectrum; there's no in-between special here. He's nonverbal with a crash helmet, diapers, a weighted backpack, seizures and he flaps along all the way to the bus.

It's funny now that Dominic rides the short bus, I see them everywhere. I think I counted seven short buses today while running errands. Not a lot of helmet-sporting special kids on the short bus. I did make a note of that. Dominic must be very special in order to "get to" wear the helmet.

Things don't come easy with autism: services, friends, patience, understanding, time, health, I could go on and on. When I'm not fighting the autism fight, I'm fighting about autism or for some kind of autism or special needs assistance. My life is made up of fighting about Dominic's autism symptoms and debating about the severity and complexity of his case. It's all so exhausting. Even I get tired of arguing and I happen to be really good at it. I'm finding that nothing comes easy. Services don't come easy, even if they are available and entitled. I'm finding that people who provide these types of services for a living do the very bare minimum, even when it concerns writing goals in school or giving an assessment report. I'm finding that like the military, our public educational system and special needs agencies have a code *of "don't ask, don't tell."*

I'm finding that the people offering these services have no problem trying to retract a service put into place in writing in an IEP and waiting for the over-tired parent to catch it. I'm finding that there are so many other resources out there and available but never offered upfront, such as physical therapy, a behaviorist, free diapers, Medi-Cal, outside parent networks, respite hours, etc. What you as a parent have to do is heavily research these things or hear about them by word of mouth from another parent who had to find out the hard way and then demand them. Then, suddenly, all these services are available.

I'm finding that organizations like nursing agencies don't know what the hell they're doing or how to keep track of someone's respite and daycare hours because *twice* now, they've let our hours expire, which I end up paying for even though I've lost them.

Autism is big business just like any other business and there are definitely professionals who prey on the misfortunes of families who are holding onto hope. The small things that make my life easier are things I would have never imagined. A short bus with a friendly bus driver, a great Special Ed Teacher with a positive outlook and a kind, dependable nurse go a long way.

Fighting against autism at home every day with Dominic is hard enough, but when you have to constantly fight for help, it becomes stressful and a waste of energy. It's like doing a puzzle for hours and hours and finding out you are one piece short.

I love that Dominic is getting some excellent autism services, don't get me wrong, but with so many agencies involved, there seems to be nothing but meetings and follow-ups and in-home visits. For months, I had aids in the house, and when I'm not having a meeting about Dominic, I'm having a meeting at the school for my older son. So there are the appointments with the aids and then there are the meetings with supervisors of the aids. Then there are meetings with the regional center and meetings with the teachers, and there's a meeting with the nursing agency to determine if these services are needed or can be continued. So now, we're gearing up for another meeting about the meeting about whether an addendum needs to be written so we can meet about that. I have to fit this all in, in my spare time. It's time that I have so little of already to rehash more of the same just to keep things status quo.

I received some great advice the other day from one of my online friends who also has a special needs child. She told me not to drive myself crazy with all the different appointments, therapies, doctors, counseling, support groups, etc. She said to give myself some room to breathe. It is okay to say no thank you to a therapy appointment or two, PT, OT, speech, etc for Dominic. Don't feel guilty if you don't take advantage of every single opportunity in the form of helping him develop something….or catch up….or learn something. She's right. Sometimes it's too much to handle and juggle, and at some level it's not helping if I am a stress case running from meeting to meeting and appointment to appointment. It's not the way to take care of myself or anyone else in my family.

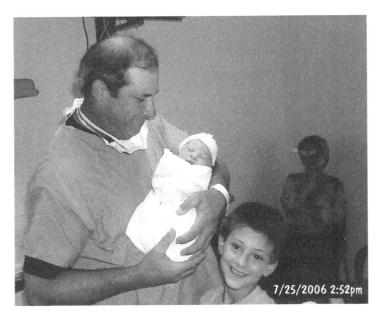

The day Dom was born – July 25, 2006.

Dom cried most of his babyhood—and in this
photo happened to be giving me the "bird".

Dom in a rare, happy moment with his older brother, Jimmy.

Jim, Jimmy and Dom, months before
we knew there was anything "wrong".

Dom had (and has) two emotions: really happy or really upset.

Dom at 1 year old.
I had no idea
what was to come.

Besides the sensory overload, Dom loves the beach.

Dom in his black socks and angel wings. This photo helps me to have hope.

Our family 2010.

Dom, in protest,
impatiently waiting for
a late bus (1st grade).

Dom on a good day, age 6.

Me and Dom 2011, wishing I had an operating manual for him.

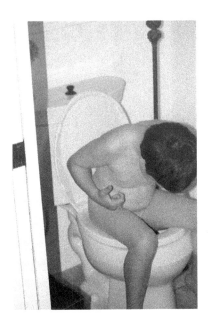

Dom attempting
to potty train.

Me and Dom 2012.

Our last trip to Disneyland before they changed the "disability pass policy".

A social media movement created by the kids at big brother Jimmy's school to show their love and support while Dom was in the hospital: #smilefordom.

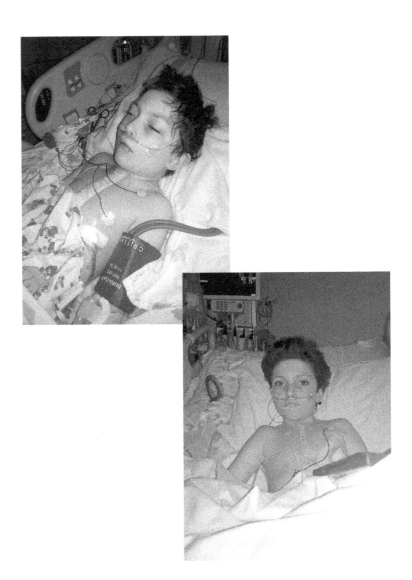

Dom during his visit to UCSF to have a large
tumor removed from his chest – May 2013.

Dom and Jimmy 2013. It's not easy being
a big brother to a sibling with special needs.

Dom – when he's happy, he can light up a room (2013).

My favorite picture of Dom, an unusual moment of pure sweetness and calm (age 7).

FOUR

FAMILY LIFE

HOME

Spring in the wine country is tricky. It rains and rains and then all of a sudden there is a break in the clouds and the sun pokes its head through long enough to remind you what it is like to have its warmth on your face. Suddenly you find yourself opening your windows to let the fresh air inside. You start taking walks, working in the garden, and firing up the BBQ, and just as you begin to make plans for a bike ride or weekend picnic, it rains again with no end in sight. We'll have a few beautiful, warm spring days and then it will be so cold it can be dumping hail. You can't get too comfortable or confident with the weather. Sometimes it can feel as if Mother Nature is just messing with us.

I had an epiphany as I watched the downpour from my kitchen window quickly change to sunshine. I thought about how similar autism is to the weather. It's unpredictable but expected. Constantly changing but always the same. Bright with patches of darkness. Hopeful, yet sometimes bleak. Stormy, wild and turbulent with heavy gusts. Meteorologists refer to repeating weather as a "weather pattern." It is common for the weather to become locked in a repeating pattern for a period of a few days. I live with a similar weather pattern in the form of a seven year old with OCD, ADD, ADHD, PDD, SPD and ASD.

We go from several days of being locked on the channel changer or iPad to several days eating nothing but Doritos and throwing things out the front door. If you ever come by our house and there are miscellaneous items strewn about on the front porch and walkway, you'll know why. Being a mom with an autistic son is almost as dangerous an adventure as a storm chaser because I have to chase after Dominic's fits and tantrums and the aftermath of his hurricane-like behavior. Then when you add in the extra bonuses like trying to cut his hair or taking a picture of him or getting him to take his medication, well, then it becomes more like a Survivor challenge. Like the weather, you have no choice in the matter or control of the outcome. In some ways, you are completely helpless and at the mercy of the storm. Some days are worse than others, and all you can do is accept it for what it is and hope tomorrow will be a better day. This favorite quote keeps me going— *"Without rain, there would be no rainbows."*

Home is Dominic's comfort zone and besides being a pants-optional space and source of relief to him, we have officially Dominic-proofed it so that he can be as safe as possible. We have safety locks on our cabinets, DVD machine, stairs, bathroom, refrigerator, pantry, etc. All our doors and windows have alarms on them. This doesn't mean he cannot hurt himself and is out of complete danger, but it's the most minimal amount of danger that we can provide for him. With his impulsiveness and lack of fear, he has still managed to break a foot, a leg, dislocate a shoulder and an array of other minor cuts and bruises.

It's a rarity that Dominic is ever just calm and sitting still. That's where our little friends OCD, ADHD and ADD come to play and never go home. He is constantly on the move and repeatedly into something he's not supposed to be. Toys? Nah. He'd rather pull the lid off something in the refrigerator, stick something in the microwave and turn it on or see if something will float in the bathtub or toilet. That is why everything in our house is on lock-down!

The pantry now has a lock, but not realizing we would need to enforce it forever, he can now reach it without a chair. Besides locks, our sliders all have tension rods in them way up top. All of our doors and windows have alarms. We even have a motion sensor in several rooms. We still have a house full of baby gates. We zip tie the refrigerator closed. We block our front door with a couch. The stereo and CD player have been purposely unplugged and the pine cabinet it sits in has been nailed shut. Come to the front door and it might take a minute while I move the barricade I have created to keep Dominic from escaping. I've asked my husband if it might be possible to bring home some cement K-Rail from one of his jobs because if Dominic really puts his back into it, he can move the furniture. He's strong and getting stronger all the time.

Besides loving salsa and taking the lids off of drinks and dumping them out, his absolute favorite thing to do is to run out the front door and try all the car doors to see if by chance any of them are unlocked. He loves to sit in the car and press all the buttons and flip the mirror down and check himself out. It's a big Christmas bonus if we've left the remote for the garage in there. He likes to get all the garage doors opening and closing at the same time. It must make him feel as though he's in charge of something grand, like a maestro. He likes to play Chinese fire drill and get out and run around the car and get back in and climb over the seats and get out and get back in and so forth. It's not hurting much other than the DVDs I find jammed into the CD player, but I get afraid that he is going to slam his hand in the door because car doors are heavy.

Regardless of which thing he is OCDing about. The word NO does not faze him.

I keep waiting for Dominic to grow out of being OCD, but I know he won't because it's gotten progressively worse over time. The OCD is part of him just like his brown hair and green eyes.

I can't fathom the joy that these odd, repetitive things bring to my son. He'd rather turn the lights and electronic equipment in our house on and off than play with amazing toys that he has no interest in. Obsessive Compulsive Disorder is just one more special gift from the family of autism we get to enjoy daily.

Dominic loves the water and loves to go in the pool, which is one of the main reasons we do not have one. He is drawn to water, even the ocean. He has no fear of it and would walk straight into the waves with no idea of any consequences since he cannot swim. Last summer we thought we would give one of those portable redneck pools a try in the backyard. He loved it, but we had to make sure we removed the ladder so that he couldn't get into it. Instead of throwing himself in the pool, he threw his iPad into it and got so excited to watch it sink to the bottom. That was a nice $500 lesson I learned, not to mention the meltdown afterward when Dominic couldn't understand why his iPad didn't work.

Wandering is a big concern for us. Just a few months ago autism wandering/elopement was a big part of the news, Mikaela Lynch, a young girl with autism, just 45 miles from where we live in Lake County, California wandered off and drowned not far from her home. My heart is still breaking for her family. Unfortunately, children with autism have a proclivity to roam and can't usually swim.

According to AWAARE, 49% of children with autism wander. The organization suggests that families with children on the spectrum get an emergency plan in place. You can download a free emergency plan template at www.awaare.org

Sigh.

Where would a child who doesn't get hit, learn to hit? Is it a natural instinct out of frustration? We couldn't be any more loving and affectionate with Dominic, almost to a fault. Along with screaming, throwing, and tantrums, we now can add hitting to the list of his bad behavior.

Dominic has one, two punched me before, and he seems to enjoy ripping the glasses off of my face. He gets pretty mad for a seven year old and sometimes his incredibly high-pitched screaming is enough to drive me insane. He reaches over and bangs his hands on the computer when I'm typing and not paying attention to him. He's kicked me when I was trying to change his pants. He throws his body on the ground, and he's so heavy I can barely pick him up. What's his behavior going to be like at 10 or 15 years old? What happens when he hits puberty? What if I can't handle him?

We don't hit, we're not big on spanking. The only time we've ever "spanked" Dominic was a slap on the hand if he was touching something dangerous like the stove or the oven, or when he has pulled my laptop down off the counter and slammed it open and shut. He does get put into time-outs into a comfy overstuffed kid's easy chair, not the biggest punishment in the world for a child, but he is autistic—what do you want from me?

I can say for sure that as he gets older, things get harder.

Dominic doesn't seem as happy as he used to be. He doesn't look as happy. I look at pictures of him when he was a baby and a toddler, and I can remember thinking he was so unbelievably hard then. Now when I look at those pictures, I remember that compared to now, he was a breeze. I'm living in a constant battle of regression and aggression. What am I going to be writing about in another seven years? Am I going to look at these years and wish for them back? At least the bad behavior is increasing gradually over time.

Dominic's behavior is getting worse and the meltdowns are more severe and last longer than they used to because he's getting locked in his world of OCD with his DVDs, iPad and other electronics. I'm torn about trying to limit them, but they are his only interest and the only thing that makes him happy. He refuses to play with toys and isn't even interested going outside for a walk or to the park; those kinds of activities disappoint him. Anytime we get in the car, he throws a fit if we don't stop at Target or Toys R Us to buy a new DVD. He's thrown shoes at me while I'm driving and screamed so loudly that other cars on the freeway can hear him. Have we created a monster?

His OCD is a huge cause of pain for Dominic and for us all. He doesn't understand how to be gentle with things and gets frustrated when something doesn't work immediately. He has thrown things and broken many DVD players, CD players, cell phones and iPads. His OCD has a hefty price tag and has cost us dearly over the years. Best Buy is refusing to even sell me an accidental warranty plan because Dominic has broken five portable DVD players in one year.

Dominic has always had a mind of his own when it comes to wanting what he wants when he wants it. The idea of "patience" is completely lost on him. He can't tell when he has to wait five seconds or thirty minutes for something he wants, it doesn't matter. It's a wait, and he doesn't like it. He really has no sense of time. I can be gone 5 minutes or away for a 7 day trip and he has no idea how long I've been gone. It's all the same to him.

Something else Dominic doesn't like is to be told NO. Autism is the gift that keeps on giving. It's the gift of psychotic impatience. My older son at this age didn't like being told NO either, but he was able to maintain a level of dignity with his impatience. He was able to eventually learn the value and art of waiting and didn't freak out or go postal like Dominic does. Even so, it doesn't make it any easier.

I think Dominic goes in and out of anxiety attacks and doesn't know how to deal with what he's feeling. You can see an attack coming on, and sometimes there is no trigger or reason. He breathes differently. He gets overly excited. He runs around the house, flapping more than usual and then he throws anything in his path. I've seen him clear a table full of dishes. Sometimes it's just because he's been told NO. He hates that word.

His teachers and nurse think he is frustrated because he can't communicate and talk. I think that might be part of it, but it's hard to tell what is just plain bad behavior and what is autism. The lines are so blurred that I sometimes don't know which end is up anymore.

Most children with autism have related behavioral issues that tend to get worse with age. For one, I thought for sure he would be potty-trained by now at age seven. I also thought he would be sleeping in his own bed. And, I've been hoping and praying for a miracle that his tantrums would get better, too. It's challenging to know what is caused by the autism, epilepsy medication side effects and what is age appropriate. I'm dreading puberty with Dominic

Dominic does know when he's doing something wrong. He knows right from wrong. He looks at me mischievously when he's doing what he shouldn't, such as ripping a book, playing in the oven, escaping out the front door or throwing something on the floor. Lack of impulse and self-control are Dominic's issues attributed to his autism. He can't stop certain actions, or he gets a little nuts.

How do you punish an autistic child who is so obsessive/compulsive when you're not sure if he actually can stop himself? What do you do when putting him in a chair or corner doesn't work for a time-out because he can escape or tip the chair over? How do you keep him from hurting himself? It's always a conundrum.

We tried getting Dominic a Behavior Therapist because around age 3 ½ the bad behaviors started to make an appearance and quickly began to snowball. When the Behaviorist arrived, the whole time he was taking notes on me and not really getting what I was telling him about Dominic. He peered at me over the top of his glasses. He was nice enough, although I'm seeing a pattern with the experts we consult. Why do these specialists feel the need to take up the majority of the appointment with how awesome they are? Why the sales pitch? What I wanted to say is, "Look buddy, you already have the job. You're in my house, remember? Now stop talking about yourself for five minutes and help us." But I didn't say that out loud; I just thought it in my head. I don't need to hear about all of the families with completely different situations and issues that this person has helped since he first decided to become a behaviorist in 1975 during a stint at a Save the Whales rally!

I wanted to keep confrontation to a minimum, but I could no longer bite my tongue after he told me not to use the term time-out when disciplining Dominic. For the life of me, I could not understand why.

You cannot reason with autism. When Dominic acts up, freaks out and tantrums, purposely throwing something on the floor including himself, he gets a time-out in his special easy chair with the seat belt sewn into it. (Yes, I am also a freaking genius inventor.) His special chair is a place that he understands and can't get up from for a small period of time, never more than a few minutes. It serves its purpose because it calms him down. The behaviorist and I had a little discussion about what I call his punishment/diversion since I call it a "time out".

He told me not to call it a time-out, but when I asked him he couldn't exactly tell me why not. He said I should redirect and not punish, and I disagreed. I said, "No, it's a punishment with some redirection sprinkled in on purpose and that is what having a time-out or taking a break in a chair is. It's a place where he's safe." A time-out is supposed to be a consequence when Dominic does something unacceptable.

How else are you supposed to discipline a seven-year-old child with autism? I'm not going to spank him, and there is nothing I can take away from him in order for him to understand the connection. His brain doesn't work logically like that. Even I know, as a fairly new parent to this world of autism, that I have to pick my battles and come up with a reasonable solution given the situation.

The behaviorist told me I should call it something else, anything else. He said it didn't even need to make sense; it could be silly. I thought to myself, "You mean silly like this conversation I'm having with you?"

I happened to see some fruit in a bowl out of the corner of my eye. "How about BANANA?" I asked. To this ridiculous suggestion, he responded, "That would be fine." Then I quipped, "If it's OK to call the consequence anything at all like you're suggesting, what's wrong with time-out? Dominic already knows that one." He just looked at me with a blank look and I continued, "I'm going to feel a little foolish trying to tell him to go have a banana when he throws a tantrum when I know that he knows what a banana really is. And, he knows that I know that he knows what a banana is."

He gave me another puzzled look. We were at a standoff.

So, I finished the conversation by saying, "I don't know that I will feel very good about confusing my already confused autistic child. We have bigger things to figure out besides what to call a time-out. You know the important stuff, like talking and using the toilet."

He narrowed his eyes in defeat, took his glasses off and then asked me for another cup of coffee. As soon as the behaviorist finished drinking his coffee, he hurried out the door and he's never been back since.

POTTY TRAINING

When Dominic was two and wasn't potty trained, it wasn't a big deal. It wasn't that unusual. I could still buy diapers that fit him. Fast forward to seven years old, weighing 65 pounds. Finding diapers (because you want them to be pull-ups) has been a challenge. The only diapers that fit him are the Goodnites® that older kids wear for bedwetting. They come in size XL which is an 8-10 boys size, which actually fit him! The problem with these is that they are very expensive, almost a $1.00 per diaper. You do the math. When you have a child with digestive issues, which most kids with autism have, it's easy for Dominic to go through 6-10 diapers per day. Even on a good day, the low-end being 6 diapers x $1.00 x 7 days in a week = $42.00 per week in diapers. $42.00 x 4 weeks in a month = $168 per month for diapers. That's a whopping $2000+ per year. Diapers are an expensive necessity that Dominic can't do without.

Changing a kid's diapers at the age of seven, and I'm not going to sugar coat it, is disgusting. Never did I think I would be changing diapers for this long, but Dominic just doesn't get it, and there's no light at the end of this subject. It's a shitty job, but someone has to do it. Next stop—Depends™.

Let me just say for the record that we have tried and tried and tried to potty train Dominic. We continue to try. And, we won't stop trying. In other words, while you're reading this book, picture me trying.

Dominic knows where the potty is. We've spent enough time in there trying to teach him. But, he has not been able to grasp the concept and figure out when the urge is coming. He can't correlate the urge with the act. Either that or he is so used to going in his diaper and so adverse to change that he is comfortable only going in his pants. It doesn't bother him to be wet or soiled. He isn't even to the point where he will come and tell us after he has gone #1or #2. He doesn't care. And, it's impossible to teach a kid who doesn't care and doesn't want to change.

The hardest part, for us, is finding a reward to give him that will entice him to go potty on the toilet, not in his diapers. He is not a neuro-typical kid. It's not as though giving him a treat or a toy is going to motivate him to go potty on the potty. He is severely autistic, remember? Low- functioning. My child happens to not want to or be able to potty train, and it's something I cannot make him do. It could be attributed to his sensory issues. He doesn't like the feeling of the cold plastic seat. He laughs uncontrollably when you try to put him on the potty. The sensory issue could also be why he doesn't understand if he's wet or soiled. He has been diagnosed with severe sensory issues. We've tried the diapers that get cool on the skin when they get wet. We've even tried various potty chairs and toilet inserts and training pants with his favorite cartoon characters on them, such as Blues Clues, Dora, Thomas, and Elmo.

Now he is so tall that potty seats and chairs don't really work. Besides sitting on the potty to get him to go #1, we've also tried having him stand up. No luck! We've tried getting him to go outside, just to see if he can. We've also tried having him run around naked, so he could become more aware of when he has the urge to go, but he has no problem peeing on the floor. We have a lot of tile in our house, which makes peeing on the floor dangerous. It's easy to clean up, but Dominic or someone else might slip and fall.

Sigh.

Can I just say, I love all of the advice I receive on this subject. All of the people giving me tips on how to potty train a child. Wow! Really? I want to say to them, "If it's so easy then why don't I just drop Dominic off at your house this Friday. You keep him for a few days through the weekend and get him potty trained for me since I'm obviously not trying hard enough or doing it the right way." Instead, I just nod my head politely and smile as if I am being enlightened. Sometimes I ask the person to slow down so that I can take notes, and I actually get out my notepad and start scribbling.

If I had a nickel for every one of my friends, family members or complete strangers who have given me completely obvious tips on how to potty train Dominic, I would be a very rich woman. So rich, in fact, that I could afford these damn $1.00 diapers and a full-time diaper changer!

Some of the obvious tips that have been unsolicited and bestowed upon me from PAGs (Professional Advice Givers) are the following—

PAG: *Just put him on the toilet and tell him he doesn't get to get off until he goes. He'll go.*

Voice in My Head: *Really? I would have never thought of that.*

PAG: *Tell him if he goes in his pants one more time, you're going to take his favorite thing away.*

Voice in My Head: *Thank you for that little nugget, but my severely autistic son does not understand reason.*

PAG: *You should make him sit in his dirty diaper so long that he gets so uncomfortable he wants to go on the toilet.*

Voice in My Head: *That's brilliant. I can teach my handicapped son a big lesson by purposely giving him the worst and most painful diaper rash imaginable. That'll teach him.*

PAG: *Tell him if he wants to be a big boy, he can't go potty in his pants.*

Voice in My Head: *Ahhh. Yes. He will surely be shamed into getting potty trained if only he knew what shame felt like. It's too bad shame is not one of the feelings, he, as a severely autistic child, has in his arsenal of emotions.*

PAG: *Make a chart and give him a sticker each time he goes on the toilet. And when he goes in his pants, then you take a sticker away. Then at the end of the week, he can add up the stickers and go to the store to pick out a toy that he wants.*

Voice in My Head: *Are you kidding me with this? 1.) He could care less about a sticker: and 2.) Not only does he not care* *about a sticker, but he doesn't know what a sticker is or why kids may think they're great, and he has no clue what a chart is or its purpose: and 3.) He doesn't care about rewards or toys. That's because he's different. Maybe you haven't been listening. P.S. He has no math skills since he can barely identify numbers.*

PAG: *That's just not right. You need to do something about that. You don't want to be changing diapers when he's 10 or 12. That's just gross. You need to nip this thing in the bud!*

Voice in My Head: *No Shit! Really?*

PAG: *Eeewww. What are you going to do about this? It's going to be a problem when you have to take him places.*

Voice in My Head: *Where's my Crazy Eight Ball when I need it? Wow. How observant of you. I really wish I had an answer for you, but at this juncture in my life, I don't have the answer to this and a million other issues he has, I have to take it day by day.*

PAG: *Just have him watch his Dad and brother go in the potty and then he'll catch on and want to be like them.*

Voice in My Head*: If it were only that simple.*

PAG: *Take him into the bathroom with you and let him see you go, then tell him it's his turn. He just needs you to show him.*

Voice in My Head*: Dominic has spent more time in the bathroom with me than I care to remember. He's seen things I'm sure he would rather un-see, and guess what? Some days I feel like using the bathroom all by myself to cling to what's left of my dignity.*

PAG: *Buy him a book or video that explains it for him, something he can watch and understand. He'll get it.*

Voice in My Head: *No Shit! We have books, multiple books on the subject and videos and iPad apps and even the little flushable floaty things that kids are supposed to use to aim at. They are also working with him at school.*

Not a freaking day goes by where I don't think about Dominic not being potty trained. It's kind of hard not to think about it when I'm knee-deep in dirty diapers. Believe me when I say that no one at our house wants to change a diaper. At this age, it's now a full production, not just a quick and natural experience. We're all hoping we don't draw the short straw on this one. We have affectionately nicknamed Dominic, "*Sir Poops A Lot.*"

Let me paint you a picture…First of all, Dominic weighs 65 pounds and at over 4 feet tall has completely outgrown a changing table. The question now becomes where to change him and how can I lift him without injuring my back? Secondly, with the diapers not meant for what is happening in them, it's not pretty. And sometimes it's a two-person job. You can tell it's a bad one when I call out to my husband, "It's a 15 wiper." Too much information? I don't care. It's the truth.

Not to belabor the point, but when you're out of town and staying in a hotel on the 10th floor and your seven year old goes #2 in his diaper, what do you do with it? Unless you have been faced with such an act of misfortune and don't want to smell dirty diapers for the duration of your stay, or want to leave the hotel housekeeper with this little gift, you'll have to ro-sham-bo and see who has to take said dirty diaper downstairs to an outdoor garbage can. Not a big deal you say? Sounds easier than it may be. How would you like to be riding in an elevator with a dirty diaper when the elevator is stopping on each of the high-rise floors? As the people get in, you watch the look of horror on their faces, trying to figure out where and whom the smell is coming from. Yes, these are good times!

Note to all of you smart, professional advice givers out there, here's some advice for you: At this point, when you know someone who has a child with health issues and/or a severe disability, and yes, autism for us, in our house, is a disability, and you can see the child struggling, back the hell off with your advice. Keep your brilliant, amazing parenting skills and judgments to yourself, and do your best to be understanding instead of telling me what it is I need to do. You are only going to make me feel worse about a situation I already feel very **shitty** about.

So with that in mind, if you ever happen to stop by my house, you will most likely be greeted by a pile of dirty diapers. We throw them on the porch. Yes. I know they are there, so you won't need to ask me if I know they are there when I open the door. I put them there and I know it's awkward. Why are they there? Because the Diaper Genie™ doesn't really work! And the garbage cans are a healthy jaunt down the driveway. And, I cannot leave Dominic alone in the house for any length of time unsupervised or he'll hurt himself. So, unless I want to cart him with me in the rain, or the dark, outside, to throw out another dirty diaper 6-10 times a day, I just leave them on the porch (in a bag sometimes), and then they get taken out with the trash once a day. And please, if you want to be a good friend or uncreepy-stranger, just pretend that you don't notice Dominic is not potty trained. Trust me when I say it's hard enough to deal with this issue every day— in the car, in Target, at a friend's house. I live it and breathe it (pun purposely intended). I don't need to feel judged or schooled on how to potty train my autistic child, no matter how great you think your ideas may be. So, unless you're pitching in for diapers, you don't get a say in this.

MARRIAGE

"Popular estimates of the divorce rate of parents of children with autism are 80 percent and above," said Lori Warner, director of Michigan's Beaumont Hospital's HOPE Center, which works with children who show signs of autism. "Parents of children with autism are at higher risk for anxiety and depression," Warner said.

I have to agree with both of those statements. Autism puts a strain on your marriage, especially if one person feels like they are taking on the brunt of the care and the other one doesn't help out so much. Or care as much. Or get involved as much.

My husband, Jim, is very helpful when he's home, but he works in the construction industry and sometimes is out of town for weeks on end. I'm home with my kids, alone a lot although my mom and her husband help us out. They live on the property with us when they aren't traveling and I wouldn't be able to manage without this extra coverage, and I know that many families aren't as fortunate.

One night, during a rare date night—my husband told me we don't tell each other we love each other enough. We know that we love each other, and since we are usually living in crisis mode, taking things day by day, we forget to tell each other. It's essential to continue to say those three little words in our marriage, to be able to look at each other and remember why we got married in the first place, before all of the pandemonium and madness of autism begrudgingly crept in.

The importance of three little words, I love you, is huge. It's amazing to me how simple those three little words roll off my tongue when it comes to my kids. My kids can be sitting there, doing nothing and I look at them and have an overwhelming feeling of love and light. It's harder sometimes with my husband. Not that I don't love him; it's just that I don't say those three little words easily and often because I'm so triggered with stress.

It's important to make time for your marriage even when you're too exhausted to shower. If you both shut down, the end will be inevitable. It's amazing to see the type of parent who sticks around to help raise their special needs children. They could easily justify that this is not what they signed up for, go out for a loaf of bread, and never come back!

The other day, I bought myself and my marriage a little gift— the gift of time, aka a housecleaner. I've never claimed to be the best housekeeper in the world. When I was growing up, I used to do the dishes "wrong" so that my mom wouldn't ask me to do them anymore.

Even as an adult, I used to hide dirty dishes in the oven. You know, to let something "soak." One time, I turned the oven on to preheat it and forgot I had some plastic ware inside. A seriously toxic fire of molten hot Tupperware started to blaze in my oven. The fire department came with blaring sirens because a neighbor called after noticing the billowing black smoke.

My mom helps out around my house by doing dishes and laundry. If she weren't around, the house would be messier. She helps out by doing my three-day-old dishes and washing and folding weeks of dirty clothes.

Ironically, now, I like to clean the house before the house cleaners come. I'm not sure what drives me to do that. I guess I want to trick them into thinking we're not that messy. I see them clean things that I don't think have ever been cleaned before. They move the furniture, and I'm not sure how they get the smell of dog, cat box, Jim's work boots and dirty diapers out of the house, but they do!

Some days I wish Jim and I could go back to our simpler lives pre-autism and remember how very strong our marriage was. I long for days where I was not eating, sleeping, drinking and bathing in autism. I can't remember a time now when I wasn't second-guessing my every move in order to cooperate with Dominic's behaviors and try to foresee upcoming autism issues and cut them off at the pass.

I forget things. What was I like as a person? How were we as a couple, back in the days of spontaneity? How did our life look before we had to anticipate every move we made and how it was going to affect Dominic and his autism?

I still look at my husband and see the man I married looking back at me. I still love, honor and cherish him. I still find him incredibly strong, tall, dark and handsome. I can remember camping and boating together and the butterflies I used to get in my stomach when I would see him. I remember him reading John Grisham novels to me aloud and quoting country music songs that made him think of me. It's not enough to just remember—I must show him and let him know that I remember and still feel the same way I did about him, 20+ years ago when we met and fell in love.

In so many ways the autism has broken apart our marriage and family, yet in so many ways it has made us stronger and more grounded with what is truly important—each other. And, all we really have at the end of an exhausting, hard and disappointing day is one another. Besides our deep love and commitment to each other, we will forever have autism connecting us.

THE "OTHER" SON

Having a sibling with special needs can't be easy. As much as I worry about Dominic and his health and development, I have to stop myself sometimes and count my blessings and remember that I have another beautiful son, Jimmy. He's my "other" son. I am grateful to have my two amazing boys, even though one has it very hard. Unlike some, I am fortunate to have both types of children, a special needs and a neuro-typical child.

Dominic has an older brother who is 13, and it's a gift to be able to raise him. He's a considerate and polite teenager where Dominic is concerned. Every day when I pick up Jimmy from school, the first thing he says to me is, "How is Dominic doing today?"

I remind myself to tell Jimmy, if ever I seem like I do not care about the little things he is doing, it is not the case. I care a lot. I have to remind myself with all of the confusion and chaos of having a medically fragile child with autism, that I must do my best to be present for Jimmy.

With so much focus on Dominic, I'd hate for Jimmy to feel like he is second. But the truth is, Dominic takes so much more of my time and energy, sometimes I don't feel like I have much left to give to my older son.

Jimmy is a wonderful big brother to Dominic, even on Dom's hardest days. It's got to be especially difficult to be a sibling of a special needs child. Jimmy is patient, loving and kind. I couldn't ask for much more from him.

For a while Jimmy and Dominic were attending the same grade school. Most kids Jimmy's age would ignore and be embarrassed by their special brother if they saw them getting ready to board a short bus at their school. Not Jimmy. He greeted his little brother with open arms and hugs. Sometimes during recess he and his friends would pop over to the special ed class just to check on Dominic and say hello.

Dominic's teacher called me one day to tell me how cool she thought it was that Jimmy and his friends were so nice. It was one of my proudest moments as a mom. He's a great big brother to him, and he is really protective of Dominic. Having a special needs brother has taught Jimmy to be more tolerant and patient. There's a boy in Jimmy's class that gets teased a lot and Jimmy comes home and tells me how it bothers him. He sticks up for him because the boy isn't very good at standing up for himself.

I'm so consumed with Dominic and his lack of progress and development that I sometimes forget to acknowledge Jimmy's accomplishments. I expect so much from him, and it's not always fair. He's had to deal with a lot for a 13 year old, and he's been forced to grow up pretty fast since he's had to take care of himself because Dominic needs so much extra care.

An unfortunate dynamic of our family is the way it has become divided. It's as if Jimmy is the product of a split marriage because Jim and I have to split up our time with him. Either Jim stays home with Dominic while I go somewhere with Jimmy, or I stay home with Dominic while Jim and Jimmy go do something together. It's rare that we all three or four do something together as a family. I imagine it must feel kind of the same to Jimmy, almost as if his parents are separated or divorced.

My husband and I do our best to make time for Jimmy. We want to spend special time with just him on our attempts at mini-vacations. When we went to Disneyland last year, we brought my mom and stepfather to help with Dominic. We carved out "Jimmy Time" so that just the three of us could have some quality time together. We went on the big rides and focused on what Jimmy wanted to do. Once I got over the guilt of leaving Dominic, we had a great time.

But on that vacation to Disneyland, I was so used to the chaos of being with an autistic child that I wasn't sure what to do with myself without Dominic around to worry about. It felt odd and vacant, like I was forgetting something. And it didn't help that every little boy I saw I thought of Dominic. Every screaming, tantrum-throwing kid I heard, I thought of Dominic. Every sleepy-eyed child I watched snoozing peacefully in a stroller with giant mouse ears, I thought of Dominic. I had the feeling all day like I had forgotten something and felt a strange emptiness in my heart.

I'm so grateful that I had seven years of just Jimmy. For seven years he had both of his parents all to himself, just like an only child. He lived in a mostly stress-free environment with happy parents and he went places with both of us. I hope he never forgets that. I hope he never feels like he was just "the other son."

FRIENDS LIKE THESE

Autism is a very lonely disease. It's not just lonely for the person with autism, but also the family and caregivers. Friends used to ask how I was doing, although I felt like it was mostly a rhetorical question. Sometimes I didn't have the energy to talk about how I really was, so I'd lie. "Great!" I'd say, forcing a smile, moving the conversation over to them.

I read on the internet that the average person tells 4 lies a day or 1,460 lies in one year. That's 87,600 lies by the time they are 60 years old. And the most common lie is, "I'm fine." I started thinking about how many lies a parent with a child with special needs must tell if those statistics apply to the average person.

It's okay to feel alone even when you have created a cocoon to protect yourself from outsiders. Unfortunately, sometimes the people you need protection from the most come in the form of a friend or family member. You know who your true friends are when you're a parent of a special needs child. Invitations stop rolling in. The phone stops ringing. The protective yet understanding parts of me get it that bringing a nonverbal autistic child in a helmet with a seizure disorder and behavioral issues greatly impacts the mood at a potluck!

Taking Dominic to a party is like showing up with an unruly pink elephant in the room. I'm usually chasing my pink elephant around because he is stimming and OCDing. The new sounds, new environment, and new people are over-stimulating for him. No one will have fun, especially Dominic. So, before you decide to lecture me on how I am "keeping Dominic hidden away from people," think again. Overwhelming social functions are not doing Dominic any favors when he's in full freak-out mode. These situations make him even more discombobulated and anxious and prone to hurting himself.

My pink elephant has a sixth sense in the form of telepathy. He's a cunning opportunist and knows exactly when and how to push the right buttons. He knows that I cannot react the same way to him when we are in public that I can when we are at home. He's smart enough to know that his time-out chair is nowhere in sight, and he will take that as an opportunity to act out. I've left several parties in tears, asking myself why I bothered to go because it is a cruel reminder of how much my life has really changed. We're no longer normal; we don't blend in. We're now the entertainment.

I'm not one of those autism moms who force my child into situations and events for the sole purpose of making a point that we have the "right" to be there. I don't feel any sense of entitlement to be somewhere with my son if he is acting out because it's our constitutional right, whether it be in a restaurant, at a party or on an airplane. It's better and easier to stay home. I'm very cognizant of our limits.

I get it about parties and not knowing what to say about the kid in the helmet or how awkward it might be to try to pretend not to notice. I don't get, however, the staring out of morbid curiosity. It's a look I know too well, and sometimes these painful moments are too much to take. How do I know? Because before I had a child with special needs, I was that person. I was that person so very grateful to not have to deal with "that" while silently judging the situation. I'm being anything but righteous now, and I've learned to accept our new reality; it's nice to be invited places, even if we have to turn down the invitations.

What about reaching out to a friend who is having a hard time? Does my child with autism now mark me? Is "Man, what a bummer, thank God it's not me" all that people see now when they look at me? I know that I am a package deal with my challenging sixty five pound screaming sidekick. But, besides the lack of invites, my phone isn't exactly ringing. Although I should be grateful we don't have those people pretending to care calling and wasting my time, the fact is, no one calls.

I take some responsibility. Life-changing circumstances, such as autism, can make it uncomfortable for people to want to be around you. I'm not a victim, nor is my son. It's just as much my responsibility to shelter Dominic from friends, family and strangers so that he's not that pink elephant in the room. I have proactively and purposely removed myself from uncomfortable situations in public. I figure that I have enough uncomfortable situations in my own home dealing with autism. So, why do I need to build an audience?

How do you know when it's time to weed your garden of friends and move on? Sometimes you don't have to do anything at all. They'll do it for you with their blatant absence.

One by one I cut contact with and even un-friend-ed supposed friends on Facebook and other areas of my life. Here are some examples of a blatant lack of compassion: judging me and our situation behind my back; never reaching out during our many hospital stays at the very hospital where you work, putting your same age child as Dominic on the phone to talk to me so that I could hear him/her speak in full sentences and sing songs when my son couldn't speak at all; constantly using the "R" word in every conversation, completely oblivious to the fact that it might be offensive to me and just wrong in general to call people or things retarded. Those people aren't my true friends, and it took some deep soul searching to realize that and muster up the strength to let them go.

Not that I am putting my friends to the test, but Dominic and our family have gone through some pretty tough, scary, and unbelievably hard times in the last six years or so, medically and emotionally. It's been pretty clear to me which friends could rise to the occasion and which ones couldn't all by their actions or lack thereof.

At my age it's hard to make new friends, especially given my unique circumstances. I don't go many places where I can meet and socialize with new people. My life is pretty much lived in a five-mile radius from my house. I take Jimmy to and from school, go to the grocery store, and run errands, like going to Starbucks, the gas station or to the bank.

Even meeting other moms with children with special needs can be disappointing sometimes. The challenge is that, even though they are the ones who understand the most, they are in the same boat as I am with a stressful life, limited time and little support. There is no luxury of extra time in between speech, special education, doctors' appointments, and therapies to be able to drop everything to meet for a cup of coffee.

Even simple things like talking on the phone are now an ordeal I dread. I can never focus on the person on the other line since Dominic screams so much. It must be so annoying to call my house and listen to the white noise of chaos, screaming, and things breaking in the background while trying to have a conversation with me.

People think I must love Mariah Carey. For the record, I'm actually not a huge fan, especially after watching her on American Idol. But, some ASD kids have an undeniable sound—they make it in a repetitive fashion as they do stimming, as in when they're flapping, happy, sad, over stimulated or just bored. Even though Dominic is nonverbal it doesn't mean he doesn't make any sounds. He grunts, screams, cries and screeches a lot. He doesn't speak words or make purposeful sounds; it's just random Dominic sounds. He has two types of sounds—good, happy screeching and the bad, angry or sad screeching/crying/screaming. We can tell them apart because we know him by now—but visitors or outsiders get confused so I have to explain the sounds to them. When I'm on the phone with someone it's especially confusing as to what that sound is, especially since the person on the other end may not know we have a child with autism. So when I get asked, "What is that sound?" I simply reply, "It's Mariah Carey." "Oh." they'll respond. No more questions asked.

I'm not exaggerating about the screaming. Dominic screams every day, sometimes all day long. I love the note that Dominic was sent home with on his first day of 2nd grade this year. This is what it said on his *Things I did at school today paper*— sang songs, read a story, followed my schedule, screamed a lot and threw stuff. I can't wait to scrapbook it.

Since the autism spectrum is so individualistic, it's hard to find mutual friends who may have a child that is the same age and with the same level of issues. Autistic families are only connected because we all have the same exact look of exhaustion, pain, and confusion on our faces. You can pick us out of a crowd! I can easily spot one of my "own" at the grocery store or the park. Kind gestures like holding the door for a parent with a kicking and screaming kiddo or assisting with picking up a knocked over store display are demonstrated. Knowing, encouraging and empathetic looks are exchanged instead of trying to make small talk with the caregiver as they swiftly exit in one piece, high-tailing it for the car. Only an inexperienced person with special needs would think it might be a fitting time to ask me what I think caused the autism in the heat of a tantrum.

I would encourage anyone with a child with special needs to find "your people." Sometimes it helps to join a local parent support group. It's completely different talking to someone and knowing that what you are saying is being heard loud and clear. The best part is that there is a level of empathy that others cannot comprehend unless they've lived it. It's especially nice not to feel judged and have to choose your words carefully or not mention something because it's weird, embarrassing, or scary.

When I'm around people who have a child with special needs, I sometimes feel at ease to just be me, the Angela who happens to have an autistic son and a nerve-wracking, unpredictable life filled with worry and about a hundred other emotions. I can relax knowing I do not have to make excuses or try to help someone understand why Dominic is the way he is or acts the way he does. I can cry if I want to. The pressure is off momentarily. I get to be witness to someone else's personal struggles with their child as well. An encounter like this can help me feel free.

If you're a new parent with a child with special needs, like it or not, autism is your new world unless you are one of the lucky ones who think you can cure him or her. As a member of this club you belong to, all I can do to make you feel better is to say with all my heart, "Welcome! It's not a temporary membership."

As much as I've hoped that one day there will be a cure or that Dominic will magically get better, I have prepared myself for the fact that nothing will get better. My life in Autism Land is now lived in survival mode. I can accept that. It doesn't mean I'm giving up; it just means I'm getting on with my life in a new way with new friends. At the end of the day, we all live under the same sun and sky.

I know the consequences and toll it takes to have a friend with a child with special needs. It's a lot of work. I'm a lot of work. The intention isn't to alienate you or scare you into asking the right questions or bully you into being a certain way. My purpose is to create dialog, not rules and to foster awareness in case you're new to the demands of special needs and what it means to be friends with me.

We all put our foot in our mouths sometimes. We're human and we make mistakes. I have a friend who insists on using the word retard/retarded over and over—sometimes several times a day. I know she doesn't mean to harm me, but that word cuts like a knife. I bite my tongue, and I let it go, and I remember all of the other ways she is a good friend to me, instead of only dwelling on this one repetitive, insensitive comment.

The best advice I can give you is to be a good friend is to be a good listener. Act interested and be there for that person without any unsolicited advice, righteousness or judgment on the loaded subject of autism. All I want from my friends is to feel genuinely heard and cared for. As with any kind of neuro-typical or special needs person, practice tolerance, patience, and acceptance. I have to do the same for you.

I'm not the same person I used to be. I'm not as easy going, and my patience with people in general has diminished. I don't have time for games and insults. So I usually tell it like it is. When Dominic was first diagnosed on the spectrum, my friends called me and wanted the shocking and gory details. Bad news travels fast, and it sure gave people something to talk about. Other than the initial check-in and wanting to know the particulars, I didn't hear from many of those people, whom I had always considered my friends, when the going got tough.

When my phone stopped ringing and the invitations stopped coming, did my feelings get hurt? Absolutely. Did I take it personally? Absolutely. There's a big difference between being alone vs. being left alone. I'm not saying it's anyone's fault. My friends must have seen a change in me; a darker more depressed person was emerging, and who wants to be walking on egg shells around that? I turned into a buzz-kill, a real fun-wrecker, always checking my watch, the first one to leave, canceling plans at the last minute, or preoccupied with Dominic the entire time.

It has become harder to cut loose like I used to. For example, how can I go out drinking and dancing when I have to race home to care for Dominic and give him his seizure medication? I can't help that my life is not happy-go-lucky anymore.

It feels a little odd to be around people with neuro-typical children. I can't describe the feeling exactly. The feeling is a combination of envy, jealousy, perplexity and a drop of awkwardness. I hate the way I feel around normal children, so now you can add shame and guilt to my list. Watching neuro-typical kids playing independently, conversing, and behaving makes me crazy and sad. It's especially hard to watch kids younger than Dominic do so much more. It breaks my heart. To hear them converse with ease makes me long to hear Dominic's voice.

It's not very often we get invited to birthday parties or celebrations. We don't even get invited to our own family's kid's birthdays, let alone grown up birthday parties, and you would think it would be the polite thing to do to at least extend the invite, knowing we probably won't come but also knowing we have a calendar and a computer and you know that we know when a family birthday is coming up. We used to get invited before the diagnosis back when it was easy and I was fun. But hey! It sure is great seeing all those pictures you post on Facebook! Looks like you all had a super time and the cake really looked delicious! Kids can be mean but their parents can be even meaner.

The sad thing is even my other neuro-typical son doesn't get invited to birthday parties. What did he ever do? Is he guilty by autism association?

We've been left out of so many things that I no longer take it personally. I know it's not fair to your normal kids to have to invite the special kid, just because he's related. There's no unwritten rule that you need to be politically correct or accommodating. It will get weird and awkward and you'll have to explain to everyone who the giant nonverbal autistic kid trying to jam a DVD into the slot between the cutting board and the counter is. You won't have to introduce me. I'll be the one running around, shadowing my special kid, trying to keep his dirty hands off the cake and yelling at him not to eat the candles or lick and put the chips back in the bowl. So, it will be pretty obvious who I am when I'm sweeping up broken glass. It's kind of nice in a way. It saves me some of the hard work. I used to spend a fortune all year on gifts for other kids back when the invites were rolling in. I like that we don't have to pretend. You don't have to pretend to include us, and I don't have to pretend to enjoy myself. Win/Win.

I also get that it's not a birthright to have friends. Dominic doesn't have any friends, and I wonder if he'll ever know what it feels like to have one. As much fun and friendship that he is missing out on, I don't have to worry about him getting his heart broken or know what being let down by someone you thought was your friend feels like. Right now, it's safe. Our immediate family, including grandma and papa, are all Dominic connects with, and we will always be here for him—fingers are crossed on this one.

How can Dominic make friends when he has no interest in other kids or in playing with them? He goes to a special day class where there are around 10 special kids his age, but he looks right through them. He probably thinks of them more as an inconvenience, if anything.

Because of their presence, it's taking longer to get to his turn. Unless you have something to offer Dominic, he is bored with you. Give him a new DVD, change the batteries in the remote, have a bag of Cool Ranch Doritos, or rub his feet until he falls asleep, and he'll be your best friend for life. Take the channel changer or iPad away from him, and he'll cut you!

STUPID THINGS

It's hard to please us parents with special needs kids since we all have varying degrees of special needs ourselves. I find that there is no way to make us all happy, no matter what. You can't win for losing! You're either asking too many questions, or not enough questions; or you're too glib, or you compare your child to mine when there is no comparison, or you try to make me feel better by saying things you think I want to hear, or you're too sympathetic, or you're not empathetic enough. It's a fine line. I admit it. You're either trying too hard, or you're not trying hard enough. What can I say? I have mixed emotions, good days and bad days, and very high expectations.

Most people's hearts are in the right place. They don't purposely say things to be offensive or rude unless they're mean-spirited and have some kind of ulterior motive. It takes the ability to listen with an open mind and heart in order to figure out which is which.

Here's your list of **Stupid Things NOT to Say to Parents of Special Needs Children:**

Pity

Don't go crazy with the pity. It's nice to know that you are aware and care about our situation, but please don't go overboard and make statements such as, "I don't know how you do it. I don't know how you get out of bed every day. I couldn't do it. I feel so sorry for you." In other words you're saying to me, "Why you don't jump off a bridge I'll never know or thank God I'm not you." All of these are awkward backhanded compliments. It's hard to feel good after statements like these.

Religious Clichés

Because you may not know how the parent feels about faith, God or religion, don't go making broad or specific, Bible-thumping religious statements unless you know that is where the person is coming from or what the person wants to hear. Please don't quote the Bible to me because, besides making me feel ignorant, I then feel guilty because I haven't read the Bible in its entirety. And, now that I have a child with special needs, unless the Bible is available as a book on tape, I don't know when I would be able to get to it. So, please refrain from making the following statements—

> *God has chosen you to raise this child with special needs because He knows you can handle it.*
> *This child has chosen you to be their parent...special child, special parent.*
> *This child has been put on this earth by God to teach you....*
> *God never gives us anything we can't handle...*
> *This was your destiny from God, to raise this special child...*
> *It's a blessing from above...*
> *What doesn't kill us, makes us stronger...*

Comparisons

Please don't sit and compare your neuro-typical child to mine to make me feel better. Meltdowns are hard on everyone, and they're so much harder with a captive audience. It doesn't make me feel better, and it's comparing apples to oranges. When my child is throwing his plate across a crowded restaurant in the middle of an autism-induced meltdown, don't say things like, "When Junior was five, he didn't like broccoli either." Or, when you see me struggling with potty training my child or changing a dirty diaper, I don't need to hear that your two or three year old just had an accident the other day, too. Can you see how that is completely not the same and might make me feel worse about my situation? Your child might do one thing like mine but we're not just talking about one thing. Dominic does that thing plus so much more! So it's not the same when you compound everything, all the bad behaviors and traits together—when you tell me that your child does that too it's really not the same at all and invalidates my feelings.

Excuses

You don't need to make excuses for my child. I know what bad behavior looks like. I live with it every day, and I can pretty much tell what is age appropriate or autism related. You don't need to tell me how your child does the same thing. Maybe, to a certain extent, your child has meltdowns, but it doesn't make me feel any better about my life to know that your normal child has tantrums, too. Again, it's not the same.

Teachable Moments

Please don't remind me how every trial, tribulation, and meltdown is a teachable moment. I live autism day and night. In other words, no more teachable moments, please.

Parenting Advice

Your unsolicited parenting advice might not be relevant or even apply. Unless you have a child with special needs, you should keep your parenting advice to a minimum, if at all. Remember, less really is more.

Photos

Please don't say, "But he looks so "normal" in photos." This is a backhanded compliment, am I supposed to say thank you to that?

Guilt

Please don't try to make me feel bad if you ask me for something, such as inviting me somewhere and I have to decline. It's not that I don't want to go; it's that I can't go. There's a difference. It's not always easy to secure a babysitter for a child with special medical needs. Babysitters aren't lined up around the block wanting to take care of Dominic. So, please don't say things like: "You suck! You're such a loser. Can't you just…? Have you tried calling…?" No I can't, and yes I've tried.

Stereotypes

Please don't try to compliment me by presuming that my child is a genius or savant just because he is autistic. No, he can't write music like Mozart or paint like Picasso, and I'm pretty sure he's not spelling random words in his Spaghettios either. I wouldn't assume your son is a nerd just because he wears glasses any more than assuming your daughter is an airhead just because she has blonde hair. That would be stereotyping, the same way presuming your son is a jock just because he is wearing a Nike shirt. So, please don't ask me to tell you how brilliant and talented my son is just because of his autism. It's just awkward when I have to tell you how he doesn't have any spectacular talents yet, other than changing TV channels without looking at the remote.

Judgments

Keep your judgments to yourself, especially the judgment of over-protection. There may be a reason I am cutting my kid's grapes into halves and quarters. So what if he is seven years old. I know that he has a propensity to choke and not chew his food. It's not a behavioral issue; it's a sensory issue. If I am shadowing my son and holding the back of his jacket at the park, it may be because his seizure activity is high, and I am trying to protect him from crashing to the ground. If I am constantly holding on to my son's hand in the parking lot or at the mall, it's not because I want to; it's because he will bolt! He doesn't realize he is in danger because he doesn't understand consequences of getting hit by a car, getting lost or falling from the top of the stairs. Try to understand that there are valid reasons for everything I do, and my job is to protect my child, not do things your way or the way you have heard about from someone. It takes a lot of energy to raise a child with special needs. Imagine the extra energy it's going to take for me to defend or explain my actions to you.

Time

Some days I don't have time to do the basics, such as take a shower, put the toilet paper on the holder, or make it to the grocery store or bank. It's harder these days to make time for friends, and it's even harder to find the time to do favors for people. So try to keep your requests to a minimum. Think of how busy you are without a child with special needs. Now consider all of the extra steps required during the day to just get by and care for Dominic while working full time. I don't have a lot of extra time, and if I do, I feel an overwhelming amount of guilt about not spending it with my neuro-typical child or husband, not to mention sleeping. Understand if I can't help you move, decorate your house for Christmas, create a website and business cards, teach you how to blog, take care of your kids, re-write your resume, etc. When I tell you I can't go somewhere because I have to give Dominic a haircut, please don't roll your eyes. Try to understand that it really is a whole-day event for me and I'm not making an excuse. While you may be taking your kids out to the park to get pizza or see a movie, I am taking Dominic on a two-hour trip to get another MRI or Cat Scan.

Acting Surprised

Please don't act all crazy and shocked when you see Dominic do something you weren't expecting, like understand what I just told him. I don't need to hear you make a big deal about it. There's no need to say, "OMG. Did you see that? He knew exactly what you were saying. He completely understood you… He totally made eye contact with you… He just went and got a yogurt out of the refrigerator all by himself! OMG! He knows what a dog, banana, or TV is." Again, I don't know how to respond. Dominic has special needs and is quirky and nonverbal, but that doesn't mean he doesn't have an IQ. Things are just harder and more delayed with him.

False Statements

It doesn't make me feel better and you're not giving me any smidgen of extra hope by telling me, "He'll grow out of it… Maybe they'll find a cure soon… I heard if you did such and such, you could cure him of this." If you imagine that I am peering over the top of my glasses at you with complete and utter contempt during these moments, you're probably not far off.

Location

California is a large state and the city I live in has almost 170,000 people. Please don't ask me if I know so-and-so just because their child has autism, too. It's really a random question that has a pretty unlikely affirmative response.

The Future

The future is an unknown. Please don't ask me what I'm going to do with Dominic when he grows up. Most days I'm just trying to get through that day. And with time comes change, regression or improvement. I do not have a crystal ball.

Care

Don't ask a question unless you really want to know the answer. Avoid rhetorical questions when you're asking someone about their special needs child. We can spot the boredom on your face after a two-minute response to your question. And that goes the same for empty offers to help out, too. Most people have good intentions when they say, "Let me know if I can help you. I really want to help you." and then I never hear from them again.

Consideration

Be considerate. This means not bragging about your neuro-typical kid and all of the awards and trophies she or he just won, or about the amazing four-star vacation you and your "normal" family just went on when you know there has to be a certain amount of envy from your friend with a child with special needs. Don't you think I would give my right arm to be able to take Dominic and the family out to a non-drive-through breakfast, let alone a trip to Europe or the Bahamas? Even a trip to Target during daylight hours has become a fantasy. If I take Dominic to Target, it is strategically ten minutes before closing, and I need to buy him a DVD on each trip, sometimes the same DVD over and over. What I wouldn't do to have my son win an award, any award, or even write his first name and it could even be his nickname DOM. Seeing those three letters scribbled on a piece of paper would make me very happy. This doesn't mean you can't celebrate your child's successes and family adventures, but try to be aware of rubbing it in or bragging.

Assumptions

Don't assume you have all the answers or know about autism just because you have heard about Temple Grandin, have seen *Rainman*, or just read an article in the Huffington Post. I mentioned it earlier, the worst mistake you can make is to generalize or assume that the autism my child has is the same as someone you heard about or a friend of a friend's in Camp Titicaca. If you know one person with autism, that's just it—you know **one** person with autism. It's better to admit you don't know about something than to pretend that you know or understand when you don't.

Exclusions

I know it's hard to have a child with special needs come to your neuro-typical kid's birthday party. You don't want to force any weirdness into your party because you have expectations about how you want it to turn out. I've been there, I go on Pinterest. For seven years with Jimmy I was there and I probably wouldn't have invited a "special needs" kid to our party because I wouldn't have wanted it to be "awkward" for anyone. So, I would have done the safest thing I knew how to do. I would have just not invited that special child. I wouldn't have wanted to rock the proverbial boat. I would have just not mentioned it and hoped that the person I excluded didn't 1.) find out and 2.) care. To feel better, I would have told myself that they wouldn't have wanted to come anyway. Then I would have posted pictures all over Facebook, Twitter and Instagram with captions of all the normal kids having a great time! Oprah says, "When you know better, you do better." Even if you think that the special needs child won't come, why not give the kid the option? Invite the special kid anyway and let it be up to the family. Maybe they'll venture out and it will be some kind of breakthrough for them. How will you know if you never give them a chance?

The Cause

Please don't ask me, or worse, tell me, what caused Dominic's autism or epilepsy. Just like all of the many studies, research, doctors and professionals, I have no flipping idea, and it's only going to take me to that dark place I hate so much, the place of what caused all this and how I coulda, woulda, shoulda prevented it if only I would have done something differently or been a better person. Just because I haven't tried the latest obscure treatment that a celebrity has tried to "cure" their child doesn't make me less of a mother. I can still be a "Warrior Mom" by solely loving my child.

The Obvious

Please try to have some basic common sense and refrain from using the "R" words: retard, tard, retarded, short bus, and anything else that may be insulting (even if you are just kidding) to a person with special needs or a parent of a person with special needs. If I call you on it, you'll most likely feel stupid or foolish, and you'll look at me with that blank stare, back-peddling, insisting how you weren't talking about my kid, which doesn't make it any better.

Discipline

When Dominic is misbehaving, I don't need you to tell me how a good spanking is going to help. I can't spank the autism out of him. Physically hurting my son is not going to fix or cure anything, especially his bad behavior other than possibly making him more aggressive toward us or afraid of us.

Complaining

Please keep your complaints to a minimum. Please don't be annoyed if you see me roll my eyes or want to come across the table and choke you when you complain about how you had to drive 50 miles to a soccer tournament or how the sound system wasn't working at your child's spelling bee awards ceremony. It's not that you don't have the right to complain about things, of course you do, But, please consider for a minute when you're talking to a parent with a child with special needs how it might make that person feel. I would like nothing more than for my child to play on a soccer team or compete in a spelling bee, let alone spell something, anything, his name included.

May my above list of **Stupid Things NOT to Say to Parents of Special Needs Children** enlighten without pissing anyone off.

FIVE

THE EMOTIONAL TOLL

HAPPINESS SOLD SEPARATELY

Yes, my glass is half empty right now. I wasn't raised in a home where optimism was embraced or even encouraged. I grew up looking at mostly the negative sides of things and always thinking something was going to go wrong. On the bright side, it gave me excellent critical thinking skills. I could play devil's advocate like no other, and it sure helped me on the high school debate team. I think optimism is a learned behavior, not something you're born with.

Now, as an adult, I struggle with trying to see the good in things. It's my nature to assume the worst, even though I have little quote reminders all over my house in the form of plaques and stones and hand-painted signs that say things such as, "Pray, when life gets too hard to stand, Kneel." Painted on a wall in our living room in giant letters is the word BLESSINGS. There's a carved stone that says, "Dreams can't come true if you don't have any," a plaque that reads, "Angels gather here," and a picture frame that holds a photo of Dominic when he was three that says, "Blessings come in all shapes and sizes."

Do I believe these things? NO! Do these gentle reminders help? NO! They are there to show people I'm trying to be optimistic, and they do possibly nudge me in the direction of trying to think differently; especially the sign in my closet that says, "Put your big girl panties on and deal with it."

ENVY

I call it "bookstore envy" because it is what it feels like to relax and be stress-free in a store.

On a good day, with respite care, I can resume a somewhat normal life and even go to the bookstore if I want to. I can casually stroll, taking my time browsing through Borders with other like-minded-autistic-child-free adults. It brings me a sense of peace and a strange feeling of normalcy and quiet, the kind of quiet that doesn't require a shhhhhhhhhhhh or a covering of the mouth with your hand or the making of a deal to get a DVD with an out-of-control child with ASD.

The last time I took Dominic to Borders, within ten minutes he had set off the emergency exit alarm, thrown a butt load of books on the floor, and screamed his loudest possible high-pitched Mariah Carey scream. I'm sure glass was breaking and dogs were barking from the sound somewhere.

As I approached the checkout counter, I momentarily had the sick, panicky feeling of forgetting Dominic somewhere since he wasn't with me. I do that sometimes.

The best part of my respite shopping, besides buying things I do not really need, is that no one comments on what is wrong with my child or tries to pretend not to notice his tantrums or odd behaviors and noises. Some things, I've decided, I should not force on Dominic. Bookstores and libraries are two that come to mind, along with about another thousand places. Maybe someday Dominic will discover a love of reading and enjoy being in a bookstore as much as I do without taking his shoes off, knocking things over, and setting off the emergency door alarm. But, for now, I try to enjoy the bookstore all by myself without a second thought of guilt.

Do I let people get me down? Sometimes. Do I feel like a bad parent when I allow Dominic to eat Doritos with every meal and when I heat up his milk for him in a bottle? Is it shameful that my son still sleeps with me at age seven? I harbor enough guilt dealing with the bigger-picture stuff without succumbing to feeling bad for the little things I do in Dominic's world to keep the peace and keep me from jumping off a building.

I choose my battles carefully. Sleep is one of those battles. I didn't choose to co-sleep with Dominic for seven years because it's a longtime ambition of mine; I do it for his safety and my sanity. His bedroom is upstairs and far away from where my husband and I sleep together. Dominic's seizure activity and waking up 5-10 times per night screaming necessitate supervision. If I'm not there to comfort him, he would get up and try to navigate his way down the stairs, stumbling in the dark to our bedroom. It could be catastrophic if he fell down the stairs. Do I know it sucks? Do I wish it were different for us? Yes and yes, but short of moving to a one story house, I don't know how else to plot the course on this challenge.

Besides Dominic peeing my bed nightly, sadly, it's the best and most quality time I have with him. Just before bed he sometimes lies down, unwinds, and is somewhat relaxed. On a good night he cuddles up to me with nothing but love. It's a calm and quiet moment in our otherwise chaotic lives, for a change, with nothing for him to OCD about except me rubbing his foot until he falls asleep.

On a brighter note, since our last 15 day stint in the hospital, where he was forced to sleep in his own bed, we have moved a twin bed into our room and have been working to get Dominic to sleep in it. We nap him in there sometimes and make a big deal about it. Baby steps!

GRIEF

People think you cannot be going through grief unless someone has died or you have been abandoned by someone special to you. I'm here to tell you that having a child with autism brings an entirely new meaning to the word grief.

I'm deeply grieving. I have, in fact, lost someone I love. I have lost my child to autism. Autism has come in and taken him, not just from me, but from our family and the world. Although he is here physically, he is not here in a way where we can fully connect, understand, or communicate. He's locked inside himself most of the time and only turns to me for his immediate needs and what I can give him. He is not expressively available to have a conversation or comprehend his feelings. He's in his autism coma, and I'm not sure he'll ever make it out.

Dominic is here, living and running around, but he is not 100% present. My hopes and expectations about what I thought it would be like to be Dominic's mom are gone, and those are some of the things I grieve. I have deep sorrow for the quality of life Dominic has in store for himself, and there is not one thing I can do about it, because it's not in my control.

Dominic is seven years old. He can't speak. He can't write his name. He doesn't know his numbers or alphabet. He can't sing a song. He cannot read. He's still not potty trained and cannot do the simplest things, such as put his coat or shoes on to get dressed. His inability scares me, and I grieve every single day about things he cannot do to function independently. Why would someone think this is a blessing or a gift?

At age seven, Dominic is still like having a toddler. Cognitively he's stuck at about two but without any verbal skills at all. He has a few sign language signs he knows, but he doesn't remember most of them. A case can be made that he has regressed significantly. Caring for Dominic is like caring for a one year old. You have to watch his every move and shadow him just like you would a baby learning how to walk. He can't be left alone at all. He needs help with almost everything. He is a danger to himself and he has no idea about that.

I wonder what the statistics of heart attacks are amongst parents with special needs children. I wonder if the statistics are higher than those parents of neuro-typical children. I wonder this because sometimes I can physically feel my heart breaking and I wonder how an organ so critical to life can function correctly when broken—even if it is just emotive.

We all go through several stages of grief when we lose something we love and cherish. Right now, after six years of autism and health trials and tribulations, I'm stuck somewhere between #2 and #8 on the following list, depending on the kind of day Dominic has.

Stages of Grief

1) Shock
2) Sadness
3) Depression
4) Loneliness
5) Physical Symptoms (sick, headache, tired, hives, aches, emotional eating or starving and pains)
6) Panic
7) Guilt

8) Anger / Resentment (at self, person who's at the cause of your grief, or God)
9) Hope
10) Acceptance of reality

I dream about making it to #9 and #10 someday.

SLEEPLESSNESS

One word to describe Dominic's sleep patterns: BRUTAL...

I absolutely feel tested and punished at the same time. The anti-seizure medicine makes Dominic crazy. One of the zillion side effects is insomnia. Sometimes my husband or I lie in bed for up to five hours trying everything to get him to go to sleep—the bottle, the blankie, the fan, the hand in my shirt, the deep-pressure knee rubbing, foot massages, the *Backyardigans*, even yelling at him to go to sleep! Sometimes nothing works. He cries and whines and kicks and screams, completely inconsolably. When Dominic was a baby we thought it was colic; now we know it is autism. I usually end up with the pillow over my head, but then he thinks I'm playing peek-a-boo.

Dominic has never been a good sleeper. He has always been somewhat of a cat-napper. Even as an infant, he would always startle himself awake. Now, looking back, I wonder if those levitating startles were some type of infantile spasm or seizure.

Those who know me have heard me say a million times over that this time around I was going to do things differently. This time, the baby was NOT going to sleep with me until he's six years old. This time, the baby was sleeping in his own crib whether he screamed or not. After all, it gets much easier with the second child, right?

It just didn't happen as I had hoped it would this time around. Dominic, being the lightest sleeper in the history of babies, would never fall asleep on his own. I breast fed so he would fall asleep on the booby, but he'd wake up the minute I tried to lay him down in the crib. Sometimes I could get him to sleep on his own in his swing. For the first 15 months of his life that is where he would catnap.

Dominic was always a loud snorer, I thought—one of the characteristics he picked up from my husband. We used to think it was cute, and then he would stop breathing and it stopped being cute. It seemed as though he was holding his breath for 10 to 15 seconds or more.

I did my WebMD self-diagnosis and determined that Dominic had sleep apnea. As he got older and his tonsils and adenoids grew, the sleep apnea got worse and worse. I would sit and count the seconds he wasn't breathing and then shake him awake in order for him to breathe. This went on all night long. No one was getting any sleep with this routine.

After his tonsils and adenoids were surgically removed, I could cross sleep apnea off of his laundry list of medical issues. But, unfortunately, the sleep apnea had nothing to do with the seizures. The seizures kept coming, more and more and continue to come with a vengeance.

DEPRESSSION

I have an exhausted, yet open mind. I've always said I would try anything to help me through the many challenges of parenting a child with special needs. So, I gave therapy a go. I wish I could say it was spa therapy, but I tried a psychologist instead to see if it would help with my feelings of hopelessness and depression. Although I'm still *shoppertunistic*, retail therapy is not helping me like it used to, neither are the chocolate chip cookies and the Costco tub of red licorice I graze on in between meals. I need to work out some of these feelings I'm having of overwhelming helplessness, guilt, and sadness before I'm too large to make it out the front door of my house!

Keeping the dark side at bay is a struggle for me. I used to be able to handle so much, thought I was a bit untouchable; nothing could penetrate my thick skin. Parts of you that you never thought you might be capable of giving are given without a blink of an eye. In some ways, you don't have time for depression.

There is no escaping autism, even on a good day. A good day for us is when Dominic isn't sick with a virus or pneumonia, seizing uncontrollably, crying all day, moderately cooperative, and the meltdowns can be counted on one hand. Even without the recurring meltdowns, the other things sure can get to me. For me, some days feel like a sadistic loop of disappointment.

Each time I try to communicate with Dominic, it's a sad reminder that he doesn't speak or understand things. Besides being nonverbal, his eye/hand coordination is such that he can't learn or imitate basic signs. We've been working on the sign for apple for months. He can't get his hand to make a fist and rub his cheek with it. His brain doesn't make the connection. I have no idea what is getting through, and I have moments where all I can see is regression and it makes me crazy. I block it out and push the feelings down and go about my day. I try to keep myself busy, and my job helps to divert my attention, but under the surface, I know it's there. I look forward to bedtime, when Dominic finally gets to sleep and I can take my Tylenol PM to quiet my mind and forget. Imagine my disappointment when I cannot escape it—even during my nocturnal dreams. I go to bed thinking about autism to realize that all night long I dreamt about autism.

My depression has gotten worse as Dominic has gotten older, or maybe it's because I am getting older. Things bother me more, I find myself more agitated, sad, lonely as I feel my life spinning out of control. No one is in charge, including me.

Selfishly, I used to turn to my other son, We were really close and would do a lot of things together which helped keep my mind preoccupied. He needed me in such a different way. It would amaze me how fast he was growing up. We would have date nights and go to dinners and movies together. He was my friend and my bright side.

Jim does his thing with Jimmy, usually Sunday going dirt bike riding or a weekend of camping. And, I have my things I do with Jimmy, such as going out to eat and to some kind of event or attraction. Jimmy filled the void I felt with Dominic. We would have so much fun together. He and I are so much alike. We have the same sarcasm and acerbic sense of humor. We even jam to the same favorite tunes.

I could be having the saddest day with Dominic, a day filled with chaos and seizures and tests that made me feel as though I was failing as a mother. I could turn to Jimmy, my neuro-typical son, to remind me that I did something right. When I can't find hope where Dominic is concerned, I can feel hopeful with Jimmy. I can look at Jimmy and imagine a bright future for him full of independence, love, marriage and children if he so chooses. Jimmy has lots of choices, Dominic doesn't.

Of course, the best outings are when Jimmy, Jim and I can all go and do things together. It isn't reasonable to expect that Dominic can go, and bringing Dominic sometimes causes stress and anxiety for everyone involved—including Dominic.

Going places with Jimmy and Jim is rarely possible since we have to alternate turns staying at home with Dominic. Babysitters are pretty hard to come by, and we exhaust our nurses during the week so that we can work. Jimmy has a mom and dad at home living under enormous amounts of pressure, and then he's got mom by herself and dad by himself who spend blocks of time with him.

Even major holidays are divided. We don't bother trying to make the rounds with the whole family anymore. If Jim wants to spend time with his extended family, he takes Jimmy and I stay back home with Dominic. If I want to go visit my dad, I take Jimmy, and Jim stays home with Dominic. Fortunately, my mom lives here with us. We have a family compound where she is very much a part of the kid's lives and sees them almost every day. If, on the rare occasion where we all do go somewhere together, we have learned to take two cars so that one of us can take Dominic and leave when the drama, chaos and craziness get too hard to take.

Jimmy needs me in a much different way, he needs me more as a guide and a voice of reason. Dominic needs me more as a caregiver, someone who can give him medicine, change his diapers, dress him, bathe him, and keep him safe.

Those special moments with Jimmy used to snap me out of my darkness and make me feel guilty for feeling the way I did because I had so much to live for in both of my kids. I do know how much they both need me. Then I would have shameful feelings for letting my mood and emotional reaction get so out of control. I would feel bad for feeling depressed, and there begins another vicious cycle when you feel bad for feeling bad and now you feel worse.

As Jimmy becomes a spirited teenager, there's more on my plate to worry about. There are other things that interest him now— school, sleepovers, friends, motorcycles, and girls. I know its age appropriate that Jimmy grow up, and he is less and less interested in his family. I was a teenager, and I can remember those days well— locking myself in my room and thinking my parents didn't know anything and were ridiculous.

The house grows lonelier when Jimmy is gone at a sleepover or party, and I try to imagine our lives without him when he moves away in a few years and (hopefully) attends college. It's bittersweet because it's exactly what I know is supposed to happen. I'm so happy that Jimmy is developing normally, his incredible height, teenage attitude and all. Yet, it's a reminder that it will never happen for Dominic. I know some parents go through a hard transition with empty nest syndrome; it's not something I look forward to. Maybe I'm autistic, since I'm the one with so many issues surrounding change and transition!

Our empty nest, however, will never truly be an empty nest. Jim and I will be Dominic's caretakers for the rest of our lives. It's not that I consider it a burden. I actually cannot imagine my life any differently anymore; I'm that used to it. But, it's a troubling thought, that when we pass on, there will be no one else to take care of Dominic. I don't want to lay that responsibility on Jimmy, even though I know he would step up to the plate and be there for his brother. It's just too consuming and I don't want that for Jimmy. I want him to have a happy, normal adult life, since he has only seen smidgens of normalcy in his own childhood.

With so much unknown, comes anxiety and anxiety for me = depression. Feeling as though my life is spinning out of control is cause for my darkness. I've tried therapy, my God, have I tried therapy. The problem with therapy is that by the time you find someone you connect with and trust, and have invested the time and gobs of money getting them up to speed with your issues, there is nothing left to talk about. The issues are still there. There is nothing left except for you to vent and tell your story again and again, week after week. It becomes another scene in your special needs version of the *Ground Hog Day* movie.

I found therapy to be completely unproductive. I don't need to tell my story to someone in hopes that they will see me differently so that I can see myself differently. There is no new light being shed on what it is I am feeling and going through. I'm not disconnected from my feelings; I know what I'm feeling. I don't need to relive my story at $150 per 50 minutes with someone watching a clock, nodding his or her head with a look of concern, offering me empathy, and asking me that cliché question, *"How does that make you feel?"* I think people can really benefit from some forms of therapies. I just haven't found mine yet, unless you count large batches of brownies. It's not to say I will never try therapy again. Who knows where I will be in the next few days, months, or years.

Drugs and antidepressants are also not the magic answer for me, which is also disconcerting because I was so eager and excited to give them a try and feel better! What kind of failure do you think I must feel like when I'm depressed and everything I've tried to feel better is not working? Granted, I only tried one type of antidepressant, and it was only for a few weeks, but nothing happened. I still felt sad, lonely, and hopeless. Maybe I didn't give them enough time or maybe it's like seizure medicine and you need to find the right drug (or blend) that will work for you. I had a hard time getting past the side effects. It would be pretty counter-productive if I gained more weight, more of my hair fell out, and I began having headaches, seizures, or suicidal thoughts. How depressed would I be then? I've given up the antidepressant route for now.

Keeping with my-glass-is-half-empty kind of disposition, support groups for parents with children with special needs weren't where it was at for me either. You get me dressed up wearing a bra, showered, and I have a sitter to care for Dominic for an hour or two, the last place I want to be is at a support group reliving my pain. I want to be as far away from autism as possible, not sitting through mutually understood stories of grief, sadness, anger, frustration, and struggle. I live all of that every day and know how heartbreaking it is. I don't need validation from other parents in order to feel better or to hear how much worse they might have it; that's what *BRAVO* and the *Real Housewives* series is for, to make me not feel as screwed up. I'd rather be at TJ Maxx buying shoes I don't need and silently judging myself or in a dark movie theater escaping reality embracing a trough of artificially-buttered popcorn.

I was watching an ad the other day on TV for an antidepressant. Either the marketing wizards at Pristiq were speaking to me directly through the television or maybe I was imagining my symptoms of depression. That advertiser asked me the question,"*Do you feel you have to wind yourself up just to get out of bed?*"

Uhm. Hell yes! I almost screamed and threw my powdered sugar donut holes at the TV.

Here are the other symptoms the ad said to look for to see if you are depressed—

Irritability (check)
Hopelessness (check)
Trouble sleeping (check)
Low energy or fatigue (check)
Significant weight change (check)
Difficulty concentrating (check)
Loss of interest in favorite activities (check)

I'm always irritable. And, not knowing if the seizures are coming back or if Dominic is going to ever talk, and my inability to control these things have left me feeling more or less hopeless.

I have trouble sleeping. Of course, that could be because I sleep with one eye open and am checking on Dominic 25 times a night, especially since he screams out during his night time seizures. It doesn't help that he's a back kicker and has to be lying on top of me as if I am some kind of body pillow. I am not getting any real REM sleep and I have the dark circles and bags under my eyes to prove it.

I've had really low energy and been fatigued ever since Dominic was diagnosed. So is it the incessant back kicking or is it my constant state of worry that is contributing to my depression?

Maybe it's my weight gain? I'm the poster child for depression based on significant weight gain. I eat my emotions. I used to be thin. I've tried everything and can't seem to shake 40 pounds. My metabolism is no longer cooperating with the rest of my body. I've considered that maybe it's possibly early menopause, a thyroid condition, or hormonal imbalance because even my hair has been falling out. They say stress can make your hair fall out. If falling-out hair and weight gain don't throw a person into depression, I'm not sure what will.

I have a definite loss of interest. Working from home, gaining weight, balding, and having an epileptic/autistic child to deal with make it difficult to want to go places or talk to people. I used to be really outgoing, the life of the party. Funny. Witty. Social. If you'd call me tomorrow, chances are you'd get voicemail and that is no accident. I am apologizing in advance for screening your call. It's not you. It's me.

DISAPPOINTING HAND-ME-DOWNS

It's not what you may think, it's not the usual—where the kid getting the older sibling's hand-me-downs is disappointed and wants or demands new clothes; clothes of his/her own. Dominic would never demand anything material—other than a new DVD and that his iPad be charged.

It's me. I'm the one disappointed beyond disappointment. I was going through Jimmy's old clothes. I'm a packrat and have saved some of his better quality clothing over the years with Dominic in mind. I thought I would go through the old bins of clothes and pull some things out for Dominic. I was wishing I didn't have such a good memory so that I could have forgotten all of the stages where Jimmy was and where Dominic isn't.

I know I am setting myself up for another breakdown but as I was pulling out the clothes that Jimmy used to wear and while it doesn't seem that long ago, it was a GIGANTIC reminder of how far behind Dominic really is.

What? You're not supposed to compare your kid's development? Yeah. Yeah. Yeah. I know. But I'm only human and it's hard and it's sad for me. I can remember exactly how coordinated, talkative, smart, healthy and I'm going to be honest and say it and probably get shot, but, completely NORMAL Jimmy was when he was Dominic's size… all of his sizes.

I guess I will try to find the good in the fact that I hoarded his hand-me-downs, which represents the thrifty yet practical side of me.

I can look at the glass is half full by how much money I have banked by saving Jimmy's clothes for Dominic. If you're going to save things from your neuro-typical child to give to your special child, whether it be a toy, clothing, shoes, games, a baseball mitt, football or bike, just be prepared that your special needs child may not want, be interested or have a use for the same things as your NT child. Be prepared for some disappointment but try to see the good in the things that are different about your children.

TAKING CARE OF YOURSELF

I've been ignoring my self image for the past six years or so. Maybe longer, I can't exactly remember the moment I stopped caring about how I looked. I purposely avoid mirrors. When you don't feel pretty, it's hard to make an effort. And, the less effort I make, the worse I feel, and so the vicious cycle continues. I now save my contact lenses and high heels for special occasions only. Most days I'm in pajama pants, no makeup and glasses.

I've gotten lazy and indifferent about my appearance, and I have no one to blame but myself. I have a lot of excuses. I tell myself that I'm too busy, too tired, too stressed, too old, too fat, and not worth it. When you tell these things to yourself over and over, you begin to believe them and then what? I think that's why it's so easy to eat a tub of ice cream and wash it down with a root beer float. It's why my weight has gotten away from me.

Food became my only distorted sense of comfort in my pitiful pastime of self-loathing. Autism has impacted my relationships, my moods, my sleep, my health, and now my eating habits. The list just goes on and on.

I can sit here all day and make excuses about how maybe I wasn't hugged enough as a child, or a hero let me down in my childhood, but it happened because I let it happen and because I ate brownies all day and frequently visited Mrs. Fields. I started feeling worthless and just wanted to get through the day without a breakdown and sometimes chocolate helped. I buried myself in work because I am and was overwhelmed with Dominic's excessive and special needs. It's pretty easy to throw a baseball hat and some sweats on and hope no one notices or cares. It has become easier to think of reasons to avoid leaving the house and seeing people in a social setting.

I sit at home, worrying mostly. My job was my biggest escape. For six years I was working for an author/speaker/trainer as a "virtual" operations manager and event planner. I had the luxury and detriment to getting to work in my kitchen—next to the refrigerator and pantry. I would work to take my mind off things, but with depression comes weight gain and ironically, nothing contributes to depression like feeling fat.

I had an epiphany the other day. Part of my depression and weight gain is because I don't get out. It's my Catch 22 Way of Life. I don't go places. I don't do much of anything, most of the time, I'm in sweats or pajama pants with an elastic waistband. On a big day I might venture out to Safeway and keep my head down in hopes I won't run into anyone I know. Shopping presents a dilemma to overcome, namely that you're overweight and have to spend money on fat clothes but I don't want to be this size anymore. Retail therapy can be a great diversion when you're feeling down, but why bother buying stuff that fits you but makes you feel bad.

It's time for a change. I need to put my money where my mouth is and realize that I do matter. I am going to put myself back on the list even if I have to squeeze ME in. I'd love to blame my weight gain on my metabolism, underactive thyroid, stress level or a faulty bathroom scale, but it's ME.

SIX

OUTINGS HOLIDAYS AND CELEBRATIONS

Writing this book, including the following stories about my life has been a therapeutic release and sounding board for me to get my thoughts, feelings, and complaints out there into the world. Thank you for hanging in there even when I bitch, curse, and talk about poo, and not the A.A. Milne kind of Pooh.

> *"It's not the load that breaks you down, it's the way you carry it."*
> —Lena Horne.

HOLIDAYS

Fourth of July

When you have a child with autism, Fourth of July is a sonic boom reminder of how much your life has changed. It's a spectacular colorful explosion in the form of salsa flying and fantastic displays of emotion rather than blowing up fireworks in the sky. We've had to skip the fireworks over the last few years, for obvious reason—crowds, fear, noise and over-stimulation.

The one time we did take Dominic to see the fireworks, oh, what a display! And I'm not just talking about the sparklers and firecrackers! We tried it. We gave it our best shot so that we could say we did, but it was more of a production, or should I say spectacle, just getting Dominic in the car and driving to the fireworks show, then the actual display itself. Roads were closed, and patience and parking were scarce.

You never know with Dominic. Sometimes he'll surprise us and bust out a normal card and play along. He watched the fireworks and seemed half way interested for about a minute, but I think the noise might have scared him or even been too loud. He wanted to leave and began doing the sign for "all done." He thinks when he wants something he has to give us a kiss, so he kept on kissing Jim until we could finally leave. Part of the problem is that he loves to go for rides, and he got a little irritated when we stopped the car to get out. Of course, his older brother was disappointed because he missed the fireworks, again, another year in a row.

I know the real reason we celebrate the Fourth of July is because we are honoring our freedom and liberty as Americans. But how do you tell a disappointed 9, 10, 11, 12, etc. year old that we're going to skip the barbecues, friends, and fireworks again because your autistic brother can't handle it. In order to make it fair for Jimmy, we will have to have another divided family holiday. It's called—*Another Single-Parent Holiday Brought To You By Autism.*

I'm hoping that Jimmy doesn't grow up and resent his special needs brother for everything he *didn't get* to do as a child and how much attention was given to the other brother. Celebrating America's freedom makes me feel more restricted and powerless because, ironically, having a child with autism is the complete opposite of independence.

Halloween

Just like most holidays, Halloween and autism don't go together. You've heard of *Nightmare on Elm Street*? Taking Dominic trick-or-treating is one weird, twisted sequel I'd like to call *Nightmare On McDonald Avenue*. No patience, no parking and too many people make for an unbelievably chaotic night. Oh. But the candy! But, Dominic doesn't even eat candy and could care less about it. Had they been passing out chips and salsa, the night may have taken a turn for the better, but he does not understand the concept of walking door-to-door to get something he doesn't care two craps about dropped into his *Thomas the Train* bucket.

Dominic liked walking to the door of each new house, but he expected to stay a while, maybe get invited in for a snack, and take a turn at their universal remote. What he didn't like was walking up to the door and then having to leave. He couldn't see the point. He cried at each house!

We left after going to five houses. We chalked this Halloween night up to a huge learning experience since I was the one who binged on the candy on the way home. Sometimes I kick myself for even trying. Then I look over at Jimmy and think about how this must really suck for him. He could have been trick-or-treating with his friends. Then I start beating myself up with guilt.

How undeserved for Jimmy! He will put on a brave and happy face and hopefully not be too terribly disappointed. I try to explain to Jimmy how it's kind of a weird and hypocritical holiday anyway because I'm always telling him not to talk to strangers and to never take candy from a someone you don't know. (Does no one else see the irony here?)

Each year that we try, even though we know better not to, at the end of the night as I'm buckling Dominic back into his car seat in his unusually uncomfortable and bulky Halloween costume, I'm fighting back tears because it didn't go so well. I ask myself why I try to force something normal on him when I know better from experience. I vow to never go trick-or-treating again, but will I? I don't know if I'll ever learn my lesson. As a parent with a child with autism you try and try again.

BIRTHDAYS

I've talked about holidays and parties and how difficult it can be attending social functions with a child on the spectrum. But what about birthday parties for your child? For me, parties used to represent pure, unadulterated joy. I used to love every aspect of a party, especially the planning and the themes. I loved to decorate and buy favors and create a fabulous menu. Oh. And the cake! I used to plan months in advance for parties—all kinds of parties, Halloween, Christmas, and Easter. When there was no holiday and it felt like it had been a while, I would plan a party for no other reason than to have a "Pinterest-worthy" party.

Now, with a child with such challenges, it's become a question of whether or not to even have a birthday party for Dominic. The guilt is enormous. I want to skip it. And I know that sounds selfish, but it's a hard day for me personally.

Dominic doesn't even know it's his birthday, even after you tell him 10 or 20 times. He doesn't understand at all that it's a special occasion or that we are celebrating his birth. He doesn't have friends, which is a disappointment to me on any regular day, but then it's magnified on July 25th when we have no one to even invite—no friends, not even a cousin or family member. "Friends" have avoided us for so long now, that if I did invite them, it would just be awkward.

But, thank God for social media! I can put it out there to the universe that it's Dominic's birthday and get a whole bunch of likes and birthday wishes for him because it's the socially expected thing to do. You'd have to be a real jerk to not wish the autistic kid a "Happy Birthday" on Facebook, right?

I find myself slipping into a deeper depression around Dominic's birthday. I can barely smile or get out of bed. Birthdays are supposed to be cause for celebration, but for me it's a sore reminder of how far behind Dominic is. Birthdays now represent all of the milestones Dominic has not met and how very different his birthday is compared to anyone else's birthday because of his lack of awareness, his regression and my sadness.

Dominic's favorite part about a birthday isn't the presents or the people; it's the cake. And not to eat it, just to blow out the candles. Although, at age seven he can still not muster up the coordination of his mouth muscles and diaphragm to push air out. He loves the candles even though he can't blow out the candles. He likes to have the song sung to him, and then he closes his eyes and we blow out the candles for him. Then everyone claps their hands and then he claps feeling all special like he blew the candles out himself. So really, we're pretending that he blows out the candle. What a sham!

If it were up to Dominic, we would do this all day, every day. It's cute the first 96 times, and then I want the cake to go away. But I feel bad and guilty because he seems to like it so much, and I hate taking away one of the few things he loves. But, then he goes crazy on the candles to the point of him not enjoying them anymore. That's autism for you— a fine and blurred line between a happy moment and a crazy OCD freak-out moment, even on a birthday.

In my life of autism, I find myself torn. Should we throw Dominic a birthday party because we're parents and we're supposed to? He's so hard and no one will really come. Then every year I snap myself out of it and ask, "Whom am I really doing it for? And why? Is it out of guilt? Silly tradition? Or, just obligatory?" It's not like Dominic will know if he doesn't get a big birthday extravaganza. So long as he gets a cupcake to blow out birthday candles for a couple of hours and gets that birthday song sung to him over and over again, he will be happy until we distract him with Doritos and have to finally hide the candles. It's a dilemma because I do want to celebrate his birth and his life, as hard as it is.

HAIRCUTS

I'm a procrastinator when it comes to difficult tasks, which is why Dominic's hair goes from shaggy long hair you can put it in a ponytail to crew-cut short. I can only muster the energy and stamina up about every four or five months to cut Dominic's hair. I have to really focus, psych myself up, and just go for it. Drinking a Rock Star right before the haircut does help a little bit. (I drink the Rock Star, not Dominic). The caffeine gives me a false sense of endurance and the extra edge I need to get the job done. Although Rock Star doesn't help to steady my hand; usually Dominic comes out of it looking like Lloyd Christmas from the movie *Dumb and Dumber*, I wish I could just use the clippers and buzz cut his hair. But, the sound and vibration of the clippers are too much for him with his sensory processing issues, so I do it the old fashion way with sharp, dangerous scissors. Did I mention I am not a professional? I'm self-taught because taking him to a salon or barber would be a complete and utter nightmare.

SHOPPING

Taking Dominic out in public, especially to a store, is an adventure. Oh, the good old days of strolling through the grocery store, carefully choosing the groceries and shopping from a list. Or, the days when I could shop at the mall without the shrill screams of Dominic echoing through Cinnabon and the food court. When shopping with Dominic, I am in bionic mode, wheeling the cart through the store as if I am late for a train, only selecting the items I absolutely need and cautiously limiting them to 10 items or less so that I can zip through the express checkout line with my exact change in hand.

Feeling especially brave I ventured to Target one day to buy the little maniac a new helmet, and of course, he had to go so I could try it on him. His little bike helmet he's been wearing to protect him from himself has been hit so many times by his falls that all of the plastic has cracked off of it. It has been reduced to a sad little white dented-up piece of Styrofoam.

Here's how it goes when shopping with Dom. I know one of two things is guaranteed to happen: 1.) He will poop in his pants, or 2.) He will have a tantrum and throw things and make me regret ever leaving the house. Sometimes it's both.

Going against all principles of basic parenting 101—I know that I must first indulge Dominic and let him pick out a DVD, or it will be complete mayhem. But, I choose my battles and I know that it will give him something to do with his hands and something to quiet his mind.

He has a hard time making a decision, and we could spend upwards of an hour in the DVD aisle waiting for him to choose one. He picks one up and puts it back, usually in a different place. I often notice a Target employee tailing us incognito, doing his best to pick up after Dominic as he single-handedly destroys the rest of the store as I make an attempt to also get milk and eggs.

I do my best to keep the damage to a minimum. I have an overwhelming feeling that the guys in the security booth are getting quite a laugh over the level of my anxiety and Dominic's manic, OCD behavior.

I'm quick to get the rest of the items I specifically came in for, being careful to keep the cart moving and positioned in the very middle of the aisle so that Dominic can't reach anything on the shelves, otherwise everything will soon get thrown onto the floor. I have accepted that any extracurricular shopping is not going to be permitted. There will be no stopping in the scrap booking section or to look at new towels.

I'm usually pushing the cart at a slow run pace, never stopping to lollygag with anyone I might run into and making my way to the checkout line pronto. I take a mental inventory and start counting the items in my cart to ensure that I qualify for express checkout. What I usually do is start throwing things out of the cart, non-essentials that might push me over the limit. I think to myself, I can always use the dish soap at home to wash my hair. The shampoo gets shoved incognito next to the gum and TicTacs.

If we make it out of there alive, with no poopy pants, and a smidgen of my dignity intact, mission is somewhat accomplished.

BOATING

As a parent with an autistic child, bad decisions get made and good intentions can backfire. I get these starry-eyed ideas of spending quality family time together doing a fun outing with Jim, Dominic, and Jimmy. Jim and I chalk it up to our short-term memory issues because the last time we tried taking Dominic to the lake, Disneyland, a movie, the grocery store, beach, etc. we swore we would never do that again. I think a lot of parents with kids on the spectrum forget things, maybe from pure exhaustion, lack of sleep, and the daily emotional beating we endure. Brain cells are lost, and we become forgetful with grand delusions of how next time will be different. It will be better.

Every time we take Dominic out on the boat we are faced with an entirely new set of challenges. The last time we took him, he proceeded to throw everything out of the boat and into the lake, including lunch. Against our better judgment, we give it another shot. We take him knowing in advance it would be a short trip, just a couple of hours.

And so it went…Jimmy was all jacked up to wakeboard again, but it was unbelievably windy once the fog wore off. Within minutes of launching the boat, I was listening to Dominic scream because of one or more of the following reasons—

1. He wanted to drive the boat by himself and I wasn't comfortable with that.
2. He hated his new hair cut.
3. The sun was blinding him and I forgot to bring his shades.
4. The strap from the life jacket was riding up his ass.
5. He was tired of listening to Kenny Chesney whine about life passing him by.
6. All of the above.

I'm pretty sure it was #6. Jim was parking the truck and trailer, so he didn't get to enjoy the full effect of Dominic howling, although he mentioned he could hear it from the parking lot echoing in the canyon. He described it to sounding like an animal caught in a trap, campers and even the Park Ranger looked alarmed.

I had just lost a contact lens, and I was already ready to go back to the confines of home. But, our day had just begun, and little did I know, would only get worse. Dominic fussed while we drove around the lake looking for a place to have our picnic lunch. His sensory processing disorder didn't allow much forgiveness for the wind blowing in his face. He was unusually anxious.

We tried a few different places far away from fellow-boaters, and he seemed to calm down for a minute. Jim took him to the back of the boat to put his feet in the water. He loved it. He was kicking and laughing until he scraped his leg on the swim deck. Then it was back to bedlam.

Since it can't always be about Dominic, we tried to let Jimmy wakeboard, but Jim ran over the rope and it was caught on the prop. Now we were stuck out in the middle of the lake with a disappointed 11 year old who didn't get to wakeboard, a tormented and over-stimulated melting- down Dominic, a very frustrated Jim, a severed rope and an usually tense ME wishing we would have never come. But it was Sunday and at least we had garbage night to look forward to.

VACATIONS

Disneyland is such a happy place, until the reality of autism sets in. You realize that you're surrounded by thousands of perfectly normal, neuro-typical children Dominic's age. Some people come to Disneyland to escape reality, but here our reality is hyper real. My disappointment is palpable. It can bring me to my knees.

It hurts my heart and stings my mind to watch Dominic in over-stimulation mode where he gets so upset, locked inside the obsessive compulsive behavior with no way out. Any type of reasoning goes out the door. I look around at all the children having so much fun and wonder what Dominic is really feeling. Is he having any fun at all? I mean, seriously enjoying himself? Or, are we unknowingly torturing him with all the people, lights, noises, choices, changes and fun-overload? I want to go home and burn this experience into my memory banks. Then I look at our other son, Jimmy, and remember all of the fun he misses out on. My parental guilt kicks in on how badly I am screwing him up by letting Dominic determine and control everything we do as a family.

The rule about kids adapting to their surroundings goes out the window when you have a child with autism. Now, you work tirelessly trying to adapt surroundings to your child. Try to do that at Disneyland.

As much as I want to bring Dominic out into the world, he's much happier and most comfortable in his own environment. But, he has his moments. He laughs and giggles which makes me think he's having fun. But then we go from laughing to manic-panic in moments. He's become really bad with transition. We have to endure a rough eight-hour ride each way in the car; which is long, exhausting and miserable for everyone. I can only imagine what it must be like for Dominic. He refuses to sleep in the car and when we arrive at the hotel, he refuses to go to sleep because he's wound up, and it's a new bed and a new room. Sometimes he goes so crazy with the unfamiliarity; we think we're going to get evicted. I question my better judgment as a parent. What was I thinking? Was I living in Neverland? I will tell you, it's a lot of hard-earned money to spend to figure out we don't belong there.

You might think it's hard to be in a bad mood when you're in Disneyland, the happiest place on earth, especially during the holiday season with all of the decorations and music, but you can cut my husband's stress level with a knife. He worries about Dominic and watches his regression before his very eyes. It makes us heartsick. I'm just as bad, filled with my anxiety about Dominic having a seizure or meltdown and/or getting lost.

What Dominic loves is going on the rides. It's getting him off the ride that is the challenge. He doesn't want to get off the ride at all, ever. He thinks he should get to stay there. He doesn't understand why the ride stopped in the first place nor does he understand the concept of waiting in line. He's actually very annoyed with the people who are getting off the ride and with the new people taking too long to get on. When the ride stops, it is a full-blown autistic meltdown time, as in grab a seat for the show!

There are so many different degrees and types of autism spectrum disorders, but I've decided there are two major kinds of autism; neither of them is fun. There's the stereotypical, classic kind of autism where the child might withdraw, sit in a corner, spin, entertain him or herself for hours, not notice if you come or go, maybe show no interest, emotion or affection. And then there is OUR kind of autism. The crazy kind. The kind who can't entertain him or herself, play with toys, transition from one thing to another, the bad sleeper, the over-stimulated and severe OCD and ADHD child. The kind who can't sit still or ever be content for five minutes. While both kinds of autism are heartbreaking,

I think OUR autism is the harder of the two. It becomes obvious when we try to do something outside of our bubble. Normal families take for granted that they can take off, go on outings, dinners, parties, travel and other luxuries of life and do what they want to do. Special needs families cannot!

Even though Dominic is not a good traveler or much fun to take on trips, it's not realistic to think that we will never vacation or travel with him again, just because of his autism. Sure, it's much harder to go places. The amount of planning and packing before a trip is mind-boggling.

The few trips we have subjected Dominic to require a huge amount of luggage. When he was a baby and toddler, we had to pack the swing. And even though he's seven years old, he is still much like a toddler. We have to pack a super-size load of diapers, wipes, bottles and an industrial size stroller. We have to bring all of his electronics: his iPad, iPad mini, and DVD player. We have to bring him an assortment of DVDs although we must be careful not to give him too many choices or it can backfire on us. He likes choices, but it's a fine line between too many and not enough. We don't have WiFi in the car, so he gets mad, and God forbid a device loses its charge and there is no way to charge it! We must remember to pack all of the cords.

Toys and stuffed animals aren't a big deal since he doesn't play with or care about them, but I know to keep my phone handy in case he gets the urge to play on it. Hopefully, it doesn't ring when he's on it or he hits the IGNORE button.

We have to bring a cooler with his milk, and there is no way to really heat it up on the road unless we pull over and find a gas station where I can heat it up in an unfamiliar microwave that is too complicated to operate. I have to be sure to pack up all his medication and spoons and measuring syringes so that he can take his medication on the road. Giving it to him in a car isn't ideal or fun for anyone, but it's a part of our day. And I can't forget the Cool Ranch Doritos in the jumbo Costco size.

Gone are the days when you can drop everything and be spontaneous. Jim and I are both pretty aware people, and it's never our intention to put a damper on the other happy vacationers' trip, just because Dominic may be having a bad day. We know the repercussions of Dominic's meltdowns in public. I know how they affect me, and I can see by the looks of horror on people's faces how it is affecting them too. No one wants to watch or listen to a misbehaved child, autistic or not. Simply because Dominic has autism doesn't entitle us to take him places to have a complete meltdown in public. Autism is not a free pass for bad behavior. It's not an issue of embarrassment as much as it is about protecting Dominic and understanding his limits.

Taking Dominic on a plane because it's his right doesn't make it a good idea either. I cannot imagine him on an airplane and I wouldn't want to find out at 50,000 feet when his ears start hurting him or the noise of the plane is too much to bear, the best way to calm and soothe him— just so that I can tell everyone that Dominic went on an airplane

When we go to new places, new environments, and see new people, it's not doing Dominic any favors to put him smack in the middle of Over-Stimulation-Ville. He gets agitated, anxious, scared and can't focus. He cries and the meltdowns are more severe. He runs away from us, which can be dangerous for him and terrifying for us.

More than anything, I wish Dominic could experience the kinds of new, rich, wonderful places and events that would make me happy and fulfilled. But it's not about me. It's about Dominic and what he can handle right now. Just because I love traveling, shopping, and Disneyland doesn't mean Dominic is going to.

Options for eating out are slim. Our choices are condensed to a bevy of drive through choices or room service—since Dominic hasn't managed the idea of patiently waiting for food in a sit down restaurant.

Even fast food isn't fast enough…we've heard our share of screaming from the back seat when there is a line in the drive-through. Patience, for Dominic, is not a virtue.

Dominic is happiest in his own surroundings and I know that. I don't need to rock the boat and put him into new situations where he is uncomfortable and in distress just because I can or it's a constitutional right. It's my job as his mom to do my best to ensure that he is in the least amount of misery and overstimulation as possible, especially since he is prone to seizures. I choose to live in a bubble and our bubble is at home where Dominic is most familiar, happy and comfortable.

TRAVEL TIPS

The most important thing I have learned about traveling with Dominic is that I need to change my expectations. We have had favorite travel destinations and places we used to love to go for R&R. Traveling with Dominic there is no R&R.

It's a game of anticipation. We anticipate issues that may happen along the way and do our best to plan for them. I often have to think of traveling with Dominic in terms of "Defensive Vacationing." Think of it as you would defensive driving. Not only are you doing your best to be safe in your car, but you need to consider the other drivers around you, pedestrians, traffic jams, etc. That's what it is like traveling with a child with special needs.

With Jimmy, our first son, nothing changed. People always said having children would put a stop to your life as you knew it and you would no longer do the things you used to love to do. Jimmy never changed a thing for my husband and me. We took him everywhere we would normally go He adapted to us. We went boating, skiing, camping, went to motorcycle races in our motor home, took Disneyland, Tahoe and Yosemite trips, etc. With Dominic, we have to adapt things to him, the complete opposite of what it was like to travel with a neuro-typical kid.

If you have a child with special needs, you can save yourself some anxiety and stress by going on a "special needs" vacation. Here's a url to a cruise that caters to disabled people and special needs—https://alumnicruises.org//Autism/home.htm. It sounds amazing if that's what you're into, or if you want to meet other people with special needs. I'm not so sure I could handle a week at sea with Dominic. I would be flapping, spinning and stimming; wanting to jump ship by midweek.

Most kids love amusement parks and fairs, even kids with special needs. It's not always the child that is a challenge to bring to an amusement park; it's the amusement park itself that can be the challenge. You need to be prepared. County fairs and carnivals are harder to navigate than larger Six Flags type parks or Disney Parks. But you still need to be ready and aware of what you are getting yourself into.

Unfortunately, as I'm writing this, Disney has made a big announcement that effective October 9, 2013 they will no longer continue their disability pass policy because it has been abused by many non-disabled people who took advantage of it because they did not want to stand in line. People with handicap placards have been selling their services for $50 to $100 per hour on Craig's List to families to walk around the park with them and get them into rides from the handicap entry area—with no long waits. So a few bad apples have officially spoiled the bunch, as they say. It's a huge disappointment in our special needs community. Now there is a new Disability Access Service (DAS) Card and it has greatly changed the Disney policy. It is basically almost exactly like a regular fast pass. Now you can only use one DAS Card per ride at one time and it is handed out to each family one at a time with a return time to come back to the ride later based on wait times, which defeats the purpose of running around the park and standing in line after line with a child melting down in a fit of autism. What do you do for an hour+ each time you get a return time on your DAS card? You can't go on another ride with it? You have to wait until you use it at the previous ride.

It's almost like Disney has said, we're going to make it as hard as possible for people to get these disability passes—and with that the real people with real disabilities suffer the most. We have never abused the disability pass at Disneyland. We have only used it on the few rides that Dominic wants to go on for the brief time he can tolerate Disneyland. Even though we've had it in our possession, we've never used it on any of the other rides-the big rides with the long lines that Jim, Jimmy and I love to go on. We wait in line with everyone else! Now the new DAS card makes it even more unlikely for us to ever return to Disneyland with Dominic. I'm not going to spend thousands of dollars and ride in a car 10+hours each way so that he can scream, melt down and be frustrated with the "fast pass".

Here are 20 tips on how you can best prepare for your next trip to an amusement park—

1. Buy your tickets in advance. Avoid starting your day off by having to wait in one of the longest lines of the day— the box office line. A lot of times you can get a better deal if you purchase your tickets in advance or at the hotel as part of a package.

2. Plan accordingly. It's known in the special needs community that Disney World is more special needs friendly than Disneyland. If you're going to be traveling a distance anyway or happen to live near San Antonio, Texas, there is a very special amusement park there built with special needs kiddos in mind. It's called Marty's World. Every ride is accessible, and there are plenty of well-equipped restrooms, parking, and activities.

3. Shift your expectations. Don't compare this experience to any other experience you may have had at the park pre-special

needs. You will be setting yourself up for disappointment if you compare the past with the present. Make it a new experience and try to make the best of it.

4. Determine if you can get a disability pass so that you can cut down on some of your wait times. Some kids on the spectrum are especially impatient and do not understand the concept of waiting.

5. Travel light. You can rent strollers and wheelchairs at most large amusement parks. You can also sometimes rent closed caption hearing devices and Braille guides.

6. Be prepared for crowds and moving at a slower pace, especially if your child is in a stroller or wheelchair. Don't try to do it all in one day.

7. Make reservations for special tours and restaurants where possible.

8. Pack for changing weather. I always bring a small, compact umbrella, even when it's not raining. The umbrella can also make shade from the sun.

9. Pack the essentials. Must-haves to pack are wipes, hand sanitizer, children's Tylenol or Motrin, and sunscreen.

10. Measure your kids. I know it sounds silly, but many rides have height restrictions. Before you walk all the way around the park or wait in line, make sure your child can safely board and ride.

11. Find out where the closest handicap bathrooms are. You can ask at guest services.

12. Bring special snacks and drinks in plastic containers in case the food lines are too long to manage. It's also hard to find certain foods that your child will eat, especially if they have a special diet or are picky eaters.

13. If possible, bring support staff! When I say support staff, I mean a sister, friend, mother, aunt, grandmother, someone who can

help support you if needed, because at some point, you're going to have to use the restroom or need a break too!

14. Have your child wear an ID bracelet with his or her name, your name, and your cell phone number on it or a GPS bracelet, especially if your child is nonverbal or tends to wander. Just in case your child gets lost, have a good plan in place. If your child can operate a cell phone, have him or her carry a cell phone just in case you get separated. Have a "This child is lost" flier ready just in case, with a recent photo, description, age, weight, height, etc. I know this sounds extreme, but it's better to be safe than sorry. If your child gets lost in the park, you are going to wish you had these fliers with you.

15. Prepare a Plan B. If the lines are so crowded and unmanageable, have a Plan B in place. What are your other options? Going back to the hotel room and maybe hanging out by the pool, or going to the room to watch a movie (especially during the hottest and most crowded times of the day). This means paying close attention to shuttle times and pickups, etc.

16. If traveling from afar, stay as close to the park as possible so that you can go back to the room easily and take a nap. If your child travels with an iPad and needs WiFi to be happy, find out where WiFi is available.

17. Plan your day and get up early to avoid the noontime arrivals and crowds. If that means paying a little extra to get into the park one hour early with a special pass, do it. That first hour can determine the rest of your day for success or failure.

18. Go online and see what attractions are available before your trip. Try to determine in advance what is important to you and your child (or children). Is it riding a particular ride, seeing the parade or fireworks, or meeting some of the characters? Study the map of the park. If you know in advance exactly what you

want to do before you get there, it will help ease the anxiety of winging it once you arrive.

19. Pack a change of clothes, wear layers, and comfortable shoes. Have a change of clothes available, so that you don't have to go back to the room or car in case your child has a bathroom, food, and/or drink accident, or gets wet on a water ride.

20. Be flexible, and do your best not to stress out! Ha! That's a good one.

SEVEN

WISHING FOR
A HAPPY ENDING

OUR FUTURE

The detesting, disappointing feelings I have about autism are not the feelings I have about Dominic. I can easily separate my feelings about something he has vs. something he is. I have these feelings about his condition because I know Dominic has a long, hard road ahead. I don't feel like I need to apologize to anyone for feeling this way, especially the autism community. I am a parent who has lost their child to autism and I know that it is ok for me to feel grief, sadness and frustration that he may never speak, sing, go to college, play a sport, fall in love, marry, have kids or be able to take care of himself.

If you're an adult with autism and are reading this book, judging me for the way I feel about autism, then autism has not robbed you of your faculties. Good for you for being able to process your feelings about something I've written that makes you angry or annoyed! If Dominic could read this book and articulate his feelings the way you do, I would be a very happy mother and would have never written this book.

I wish Dominic could have been born with a different kind of autism, your kind of autism. A brainy, gifted, academic kind of autism that would enable him to talk, read, write, count, communicate, discriminate, judge and function at a higher level. Your level. You don't know how many times I have wished Dominic had the Aspberger's form of autism or even a physical deformity so that I could have conversations with him and connect with him outside of just taking care of him. I've wished for a higher version of low-functioning autism that would afford him the capacity to use the toilet, get dressed on his own, and remember to take his seizure medications twice a day. Those are my wishes, but not all wishes come true. My grandma used to say "If wishes were horses, all beggars would ride." I never understood that saying until now.

I struggled with whether or not to write a book like this. I could have just as easily sat down and written about all of the great things about having a child with special needs and ASD, all of the blessings and the gifts. I could have talked about the wonderful journey I had embarked on and how much I have learned and grown—with all of its teachable moments, how it has made me a better person. I could have called it *The Bright Side of Autism*. I might have even sold more books. People would have liked me more because, let's face it; no one wants to read a depressing story of disappointment and frustration. People want a joyful, happy ending right? But, for me, it would have been a lie. That's not my life, and I wanted to tell you the truth.

I used to be very caught up in what people thought of me, even people I didn't know or like. Having a child with special needs is like a natural purging. You no longer have time to think only about yourself or be self-absorbed. It's not all about me anymore, and I don't care what you think of me, as a mother or a person, after reading this book. I warned you, it wasn't going to be all sunshine and rainbows. What I do care about is that I know how hard I try with my sons, both Dominic and Jimmy, to give them a good life and do my best with them so that they are taken care of, happy, and fulfilled. I want the same things for both of my kids. I want them to know and feel my unconditional love, loyalty beyond measure, and that I honor them as human beings. I cherish them. They are my world, and so long as they know that, it's all that matters to me.

I have heard from righteous and judgmental people how I should feel about autism. I have been told to get over it. I have been told I'm stuck. I have been told I dwell too much on it. I have been told I need to accept it and stop grieving. I have been told I should stop worrying. I have been told it's my "old" story. Although, it's not an "old" story, I wish it were something behind me. Something I choose to bring up and relive over and over. But it's not. It's actually a new story, every single day because with autism comes uncertainty and chaos and new challenges and issues. There is nothing "old" about it other than having to live with it day after day after day with no escape.

Who is anyone to judge how I feel about something? We all do things at our own pace in our own way. That's the beauty of individuality and expression. I will get over this autism/epileptic thing when I am good and ready, and I don't have to pretend I'm ready, just to pacify others.

One of the only times I have felt validated when it comes to my feelings about autism occurred while watching my guilty pleasure-The Real Housewives of New Jersey. There is a cast member on the show, Jacqueline Laurita, who has a son who was recently diagnosed with autism and it showed the emotional toll it had on her and her family. I'm not sure how much of the show is reality vs. scripted but the emotion was really there. She could barely talk about the effects of the autism without breaking down and crying—she talked about the depression and locking herself in her house—and that was on television where you get numerous takes and have editors to edit out ugly crying scenes. They kept the tears in there, and whether they did it for sympathy, ratings or a reaction, the fact remains that it is hard to watch your child struggle. For me, it was the most real and raw of all of the storylines in any of the RHW series. Brava to you Bravo Network!

I often agonize about the quality of life Dominic has ahead of him. I'm not just speaking of the day-to-day hoping the seizures don't come back. I'm talking about how will he live and survive? Who will care for him? Where will he live? Who will feed him? Who will bathe, dress, and change him? Who will clip his fingernails? Who will count his money and buy him necessities? Who will take him to the doctor? Who will make sure he takes his seizure medications? Most importantly to me, who will comfort, hold, and love him?

The planning process usually takes place when the child is a young adult. It's called a transition plan. But what if something happens to Jim or me before that? I want to have a plan in place now and modify it as time passes.

Right now in 2013, it's reported that there are only about 3,500 programs available nationwide for autistic adults, compared with 14,400 for autistic kids. Some are considered little more than daycare, while other vocational programs may consist of participants working for a company, maybe doing piecework or some other menial production-line job. This is definitely not the life I had imagined for my son. Most programs pay nothing to the worker because so many of the job programs require special aids and shadow coaching in order to get the job done correctly. Only about 15% of the special needs people receive compensation for their work.

I went to the bank the other day and when pulling out of the driveway, I stopped and let a group of guys cross. There were six or seven men in their twenties, and at closer look they were all some form of special needs adults, except for the leader. The leader must have been their caretaker, taking them on a walk or outing of some sort. The special needs guys all had the same look of oblivion on their faces and didn't seem to have any idea of where they were or what they were doing. They were walking aimlessly, just like cattle might, not even really aware of each other, let alone their surroundings. It was sad and heartbreaking. They had no idea I was watching them so intently, studying them in fact. They had no idea why I found them so very interesting.

My mind raced, and then I got a lump in my throat. I felt for a moment as if I might throw up. Tears welled up in my eyes, yet I couldn't break the stare. I tried to quiet my mind and stop the stream of familiar questions. All I could think about was will this be my son in fifteen years? Will he be oblivious to his surroundings and going for walks with a caretaker? Will that caretaker be me? What will happen to him when I die? Who will love him? Who will be his leader? Will he have a purpose in life? Will he be productive and have any kind of self-esteem or pride? Will he know right from wrong and be able to control his impulses, or will he have to be institutionalized in a sterile and cold environment with round-the-clock care, medication and therapy in order to contain him? Will he be a violent teenager or adult? Will he ever speak? Will he be abused if not under my protection? Will there be someone who will be especially kind to him or comfort him when he needs it? Will he be a ward of the state? Will he remember me when I'm gone? Will he realize how much he was loved?

But my biggest question, the one that haunts me every single day and night is—will he be happy and what, besides Doritos and DVDs, will make him tick?

The best programs have huge waiting lists and aren't available in all areas of the country. Most of the programs for autistic adults are not specifically designed for autism, but encompass many disabilities and accommodate adults with a myriad of special needs. With federal and state budget cuts, those options will likely diminish by the time Dominic reaches adulthood.

The steep, recurring price of many programs and therapies is why raising an autistic child, according to a Harvard University study, can add up to $3.2 million over his or her lifetime, compared with the $222,360 it typically takes to raise a child to age 18.

I hope that Dominic will live with me forever. I like to use the word forever since it sounds longer to me than "for the rest of my life" since I am fast approaching 50 years old. This of course would be in my perfect, imaginary world that I have created for myself and Dominic. It's not taking into consideration that things could vastly change when he hits puberty. I'm hoping that as he continues to grow into a man, he'll keep the same sweet disposition, scream a lot less and I can continue to give him time-outs without any aggressive or violent pushback. What do you do as a parent? Sit back and hope for some state disabilities funding? Who can you turn to?

Advocates say that the needs of this population must be addressed by the private and public sectors, such as building appropriate housing, creating tax-free savings accounts for parents to use for their adult children's care, and providing government incentives to companies that hire autistic employees.

We pay a lot of money for health insurance, and we're fortunate to have health insurance but it's not FREE. It comes at a price. A lot of insurance companies still do not pay for autism-related treatments. As a matter of fact, once the insurance company learns that you a have a child with autism, it becomes apparent that things start getting flagged and questioned, even regular pediatrician visits. For us, we had a battle with our insurance carrier over paying for a visit with a neurologist. The coding that the neurologist's office used for the epilepsy kicked the claim back, and the insurance company refused to pay for the visit because they said that epilepsy was a psychological condition. After three phone calls and two letters, they finally paid their share of the invoice.

Enrolling Dominic in a private school for autistic children is not an option right now. It would cost us out of pocket between $24,000 and $30,000 per year. There are no scholarships available for middle-class families with dual incomes. He would get more individualized and intensive instruction than he is now receiving at a public school. The student to teacher ratio at his school is not great, and with so many kids with special needs, special attention is not a priority. He receives minimal speech and occupational therapy, only 20 minutes per week. It takes Dominic 20 minutes sometimes to get settled and by then, the therapy session is over.

Supplementing his therapies and services is super expensive in the private sector. I'd have to take off work to make the time to take him to multiple therapy appointments each week. We just couldn't afford the prohibitive cost.

I'm not expecting handouts just because my son happens to be autistic. I'm simply stating the facts. I don't have the resources or celebrity paychecks of a Jenny McCarthy or John Travolta to provide all I wish I could provide to Dominic and his ASD.

> *"Turn your wounds into wisdom."*
> —Oprah Winfrey

MY FANTASY

Some may say I have weird fantasies. They don't involve winning the lottery or traveling all over the world. Besides the obvious fantasy of finding a cure for Dominic's epilepsy and autism and curing cancer, I would like a solid eight hours of uninterrupted REM sleep and a best friend who can relate to what it is I'm experiencing.

The "old" me used to love to entertain, go out and hang around with friends. As I got older and had kids, my friends got older and had kids, too, so we would do family things and go places with the kids in mind. We would camp, go to fairs and Disneyland, have BBQs at the beach, go boating in the summer, and snow skiing in the winter. We could easily celebrate birthdays and Fourth of July and do Easter Egg Hunts. If we wanted to drop everything and go to a Farmer's Market or a movie, it wasn't a problem. Impromptu get togethers were conceived and planned with a simple phone call and check of the calendar. The kids would play and the grownups would talk and drink wine. Those days are long gone. I mentioned before, it's a lot of work being my friend. It takes a lot of patience and willingness to spend time with my complicated child and me.

Most grownups can't handle it when Dominic shoves his entire hand into the bowl of chips and starts licking them one at a time, or when he finds the volume control on the TV or stereo and blasts out the room. Sure, they do their best to be polite. They nod their head in understanding but the look on their face is something you can't shake. You can see them wince, share a look with someone, even roll their eyes in discomfort when the meltdowns and distractions begin. It becomes a matter of involving the entire group every time a Dominic issue hits. Maybe he just threw himself on the floor for the 10th time and is in a screaming fit only a new DVD can bring him out of. Or, maybe he just crapped in his pants at dinner. Whatever the issue is, it's guaranteed to make someone uncomfortable, and I know we will be the discussion at bedtime that night. It's not fun for a group of people and their kids. It's not like I can say, "Dominic, go outside and play." Those words will never leave my lips. He could never go outside and play by himself or with another group of kids his age. He needs a constant shadow, and people don't get that. Besides not being a social kid who likes to play with others, he is an accident waiting to happen.

I don't say these things for any kind of pity. I say them because they're our truth. At present, this is now our life, and if you have a child with special needs, you will understand exactly what I am saying, If not, and you happen to have a friend with a child with special needs, I hope this gives you a greater understanding of how you can be a better friend.

My new fantasy is that I will meet another family with a child or children with special needs, social issues, uncontrollable impulses, heightened sensitivity, no manners or regard for rule, and together we can hang out, do the best we can to cling to what's left of our dignity, jockeying distractions, while drinking wine and getting through the evening together in unison. No judgment. No shame. No guilt. No worries. Doesn't that sound grand?

Let's get back to reality. Think I'm overreacting or relishing in self pity? Let me paint you a quick picture of what getting together at your house, an unfamiliar place for Dominic, might look like:

We set a date for dinner at your house because you've been insisting, even after tons of excuses and warnings on why it might not be a good idea. But you persist. We arrive at your home, probably at least 20 or 30 minutes late considering all we just dealt with getting Dominic out the door. It's a warm and balmy 95 degrees and we're a little on edge from the chaotic car ride across town. Unfortunately, we'll need to close your beautiful doors so that Dominic doesn't escape out of one of them, run out into the street and get hit by a Buick. It's a little stuffy inside with all the doors closed and you don't have A/C, so we sit outside on your new deck. But Dominic wants to go up and down the stairs and damn it, I forgot his helmet! So now I am up and down, following him around while he goes in and out of the house. He finds that yummy smelling soy candle you had burning on the coffee table, and besides burning himself, he almost sets the place ablaze. Thank God you have fire insurance! Although, I'm not sure how to get hot wax out of your carpet, but I bet if you Google it you'll get some good ideas. And, I know you had something cooking in the oven, it sure smelled good, but I'm sorry that Dominic turned it off when he was playing with the stove. So, now you'll need to probably use your microwave to get the chicken finished on time with the rest of the meal you've worked so hard on.

I know it's a stretch for your kids to want to try to play with Dominic while we're there, and please apologize to your daughter for me, I'm sorry Dominic shoved 2 CDs at once into her brand new laptop and broke it. I'm also really sorry about your iPhone. I hope those pictures you had stored on there weren't special, and I sure hope you backed up your data. Also, thanks for being a doll and getting me that plastic garbage bag when I need it. Since I used up all of the baby wipes cleaning up the juice Dom spilled on the floor, I appreciate you letting me use that monogrammed towel you have hanging in your bathroom. I promise to replace it. I watched the look of horror on your face when you came into the bathroom when I was changing Dominic's pants and got some excrement on your new bathmat. Your bathroom will never be the same no matter how much sanitizer and Lysol you use in there. You were nice enough to lend me a pair of your daughter's pajamas for Dominic since he blew out his clothes with the aforementioned bathroom saga. He doesn't care that they are pink with flowers on them at all; he just didn't like that they were a poor blend of polyester and itchy, so he threw a bit of a fit, knocking over the very expensive wine you had "breathing" on the table as our microwaved dinner got cold while I changed him.

I have to confess, I did the cell phone trick where I dial my phone from Jim's phone and dreamt up that imaginative family emergency where we had to leave before dessert was served. But, I saw the look of utter relief you gave your husband, and I'm pretty sure your kids are doing a happy dance.

Let's just say we tried and do our best to forget the entire charade. We gave it our best shot and next time when I'm telling you it's not going to be easy or a good idea, maybe you'll listen.

I'm not the friend I used to be to people. I'm not as available, understanding, or patient. I don't have a lot of time and energy to put into nurturing a friendship, so my isolation is no one's fault but my own. I thought I would meet so many people with my circumstances along our journey, but that hasn't been the case. I was disappointed until I realized I was once again expecting too much from people. How can I expect a person in my similar situation to have any extra time for me when I clearly don't have extra time for them? It's become the bane of my existence walking a tightrope of despair and time management. I've been saddened by my new feelings of loneliness and missing having a BFF when all I had to do was open my eyes. My best friend is right in front of me, all along going through the exact same thing I am. We have so much in common. We understand each other. It's my husband, Jim.

THE BRIGHT SIDE OF AUTISM

Because I hate to be known as the pessimistic narrator of autism, I think it's only fair I tell you some of the perks of parenting a child with severe autism and other special needs. If I use my biggest imagination and put on my optimist hat, I can come up with what is advantageous about having a kiddo with a remarkable repertoire of special needs issues.

Here are my top 17—

1. Dominic has no sense of time. This can go either way, but he's never concerned about being late, nor does he care what time it is. Sometimes I can trick him mid-morning and get him to take his afternoon nap and then later, tell him its naptime and he takes another nap in the afternoon While Dominic might have a pretty good sense of where he is, he has no clue about the passing of time or having to wait for something. Jim says

he's a bit like a dog, no matter how long you've been gone, he is happy to see you. I could be gone all day or for three minutes, it doesn't mean anything to him. He's always equally excited to see me again.

2. Dominic is nonverbal. He can't talk back like most neurotypical children.

3. Dominic's not all hung up on name brands and having the most expensive jeans, shoes, iPhone, laptop, etc. He's happy with almost anything you give him as long as it's plugged in or has decent battery life. He doesn't care where his clothes come from or if they match, or if he's even actually wearing any clothes at all. And he doesn't care what I look like…he doesn't care if I don't wear makeup, fancy clothes or if I've gained weight. I don't embarrass him; he loves and accepts me the way I am.

4. Dominic is simple. He knows what he wants and likes and once you can figure that out, he is fairly content and happy. It's the figuring out what "it" is that can sometimes be a challenge because of #2.

5. Dominic's not greedy about money, nor does he know what money is. And, he's not constantly asking me for money. Other than not wanting to share his iPad, or wanting something when he wants it, he has no sense of materialism or stinginess.

6. As big of a stigma as it is for me and all it represents, the short bus is sure convenient. It does come directly down our driveway and picks up and drops off Dominic at our doorstep almost like a large yellow limousine service. God love it.

7. Because I have no social life, I save a lot of money on babysitters and fancy restaurants that serve overpriced drinks and stinky cheese. And, since my kid may not be very social or have any friends, I save a lot of money by not having to buy other kids gifts.

8. I don't need travel insurance or fancy luggage because my luxury vacations are now limited, since I do not travel with a full staff of nannies.

9. Handicap plaque parking privileges and now a very limited very restrictive disability pass advantages at Disneyland.

10. Having a child with special needs gets me out of a lot of things, not that I use Dominic's disability as an excuse not to do something or go somewhere, but his issues really do dictate the where, how, and for how long we can do something. It just so happens this works out in our favor (a lot).

11. Another double-edged perk of having a child with special needs is that I do not take milestones (or other things) for granted. The smallest accomplishment and success is HUGE, and we celebrate each and every one. I have a new appreciation for things like him drinking out of a cup, learning a new sign, and being able to jump with two feet off the ground.

12. Increased vocabulary, mine not his. I now know meanings of words such as idiopathic, paroxysm, annexation, confutative, echolalia, apraxia, xenophobic, myclonic, bombilate, regression, adroitness, stimming, abysmal, cerebral, pertinacious and many more. Thank you autism and epilepsy.

13. Finding out who my true friends are. When faced with life changing issues and chaos I have quickly learned whom I can count on and trust. Autism helped me figure out who my genuine friends were and who truly cares about us; insignificant people have been purged from my life in the process.

14. Caring for a child with special needs sure makes a compelling reason to NOT have to serve on a jury. And if the judge doesn't believe me, I can always bring Dominic with me to give them a taste of the chaos, disruption, and mayhem I deal with at home most days.

15. Dominic doesn't know a different life. He is what he is and that's all that he knows. It's not like he's contrasting or associating his life back when it was "normal" or he was "healthy" to now.

16. All you need is LOVE. Not all children with autism are programmed to give and receive love and affection. Some kids on the spectrum do not make eye contact, want to be touched or hugged or kissed. So with the crap sandwich we've been served having a child on the spectrum, luckily, this is one social skill that Dominic is fully equipped with.

17. Important life lessons have officially been learned, especially in the patience department. Having a child with autism and other special needs has really taught me to let go of the little stuff. In other words, it's given me the power of perspective. I used to stress over some really dumb, mindless, silly, vain, extraneous things, like wrinkles, grey hair, traffic, power outages, waiting in line, weather, sleep and gossip. I have a new appreciation for what is truly important in life, like moments of good health, unfiltered happiness, and unconditional love.

CONCLUSION

There were a lot of tears that fell on the day Dominic was diagnosed and many more since then. Fall of 2007 will be forever burned into my memory as a time when our life changed. Even though I already knew, hearing those painful words from the doctor was heartbreaking, sobering, confusing, and unpredictable. Much was left to my imagination.

When you're given a diagnosis of autism, everything changes and for a moment, time stands still. You don't know what will be in store for you other than what you've heard or seen on Oprah or have caught on the tail end of a documentary about it. You know you are going to have your work cut out for you, and that it's going to be harder than you ever could imagine.

I don't claim to have all the answers. Autism is like raking leaves on a windy fall day, except there is no other season coming in to give you a break or for you to look forward to. You just keep raking the leaves, trying to keep up and manage things before you are so buried in leaves you can't find your way out.

Unfortunately, for some, there is not a lot of light at the end of the tunnel. So, you imagine the worst while doing your best fighting for a semblance of normality. I do my best to try not to think about it and to block it out when I can. I have fleeting moments of hope. For example, when I glance over at Dominic and he's doing something very boyish, typical and age appropriate. It might even be something as simple as a look of lucidity on his face where I can see him, see me and not just be looking through me. Those moments are few, and because of that even more extraordinary to me when they do occur.

Autism is not a side-line or spectator sport. It requires, actually… demands 100% of your effort at all times. It's an in-your-face disorder and there are few time outs.

Right or wrong, I still wrestle with the ticker-tape of questions in my head: What if he never talks? Will he ever go to a regular classroom? Will he ever be able to take care of himself? Who will take care of him when we're gone? Will he ever find true love? Will he be okay? I get buried alive in thoughts of illusion of how I think his life should be. Sobering to realize that Dominic does not live in my world, I live in his. He does not long for friendship or relationships outside of our home. He does not have a social agenda or get his feelings hurt because he does not get invited to a party. Those are my feelings projected unfairly upon him and I need to figure out a way to be satisfied with his life the way he is. I need to let go of my expectations and stop pushing my world and customs on him whether I think they're traditional or not. It's not like he has memories of living his life one way and then it being taken from me. He does not live in a world of disappointment like I do.

Disappointment is my identity; it is my hang up and mine alone. Living a life of autism is all he knows.

When the epilepsy showed up, it knocked the wind out of me and left me breathing into a brown paper bag. I wasn't ready for it. I was too busy being burdened and devastated by the idea of autism. So, good or bad, the epilepsy knocked some sense into me. I had been worried and depressed and then the seizures came along and shook me to my core almost taunting me with "Oh Yeah? Forget about the autism. Here's something to really worry about!" Then, the cancer scare was even more unbearable than the autism and epilepsy combined, similar to a furious parent saying to a child, "You want me to give you something to cry about?"

So now, I don't feel the same about the autism. I've come full circle, from hating it as a new diagnosis but having hope to now hating it again minus the hope.

I still wish and pray Dominic didn't have it. I still despise it for all it has taken from him and from us. This doesn't mean I don't have dreams for my son. If I close my eyes, I can still see Dominic grown up and living on his own doing something he loves. I can picture him happy, surrounded by people who love him. In my wildest dreams I will wake up one day and he will turn to me and say, "Mommy, I love you," and he will talk and function at a higher level. He will be completely independent, and his seizures will have magically vanished and everything will be fine. If only…

So until my fantasy comes true, I will continue to focus on Dominic and every single one of his special needs. I will do my best to be a good mom and to make sure he is safe and knows how much he is loved despite all of this. I have had seven years to fall in love with and become accustomed to this little man, quirks, tantrums, developmental delays, medical challenges, beautiful green eyes, and all. He is one of the most loving and cuddly little autistic people I have ever met, and I know he loves me just as much as I love him, completely and unconditionally. He's so pure and although taxing, he's just an innocent little boy who doesn't know there is anything different about him.

My days are no longer filled with the idea of trying to "fix" or "cure" him, although it would still be nice. For whatever reason, this must just be who he is supposed to be. His destiny will be that he was born into this family to remind us of how little control we have over things and to teach us patience at a different level that only caregivers with special need dependents can appreciate. He has also given me a serious lesson in faith. He has taught me how to be strong in the face of adversity, stand up for what I believe in, and how to love completely. More importantly, Dominic has taught my entire family how precious life is and how your quality of life can be taken away in an instant. He is here to remind me on a daily basis of what is truly important.

People assume that it's the person with autism that has trouble with transition. But, it's me. I am the one who has the hardest time with it. Even though I get discouraged, disappointed, and depressed, I still find value in the possibility of what could be. My hope is that people will better understand what some parents may be going through and stop judging us for wanting a better life for our children. More importantly, let us feel the way we feel and grieve the way we want and need to grieve without attack or our fear to speak the truth. Autism is hard, loving our kids is easy.

Who knows what the future will hold for Dominic and our family. I'm doing my best not to dwell on it, albeit, it tends to get the best of me. I have good days and bad days. On my darkest days, what pulls me out of my funk is remembering that Dominic did not ask to be born. I chose to bring him into our lives and be his mom, which means I have to be the best mama to him that I possibly can, despite any tantrum, shortcoming, challenge, and issue (health of otherwise).

Our story, thus far, has no astonishing and notable happy ending. There is no internet link to a video gone viral on YouTube where you will be amazed and moved to tears by the special kid with autism playing in the final minute of a game and making an unlikely basket. There is no inspiring guest appearance on Katie Couric or Ellen to talk about the remarkable gifts or abilities of autism. There is only me telling you my truth and doing the best I can, one day at a time.

People always ask me if I have learned acceptance throughout this journey that mostly feels like a test. I tell them no, because part of me feels like I need to constantly hate it, fight it and fix it. Somewhere in my mind, I feel like if I accept Dominic's disabilities I am ultimately giving up on him. It doesn't make me a bad mother to wish a better, easier and healthy life for Dominic or to want to take his pain away.

Do I accept autism? Yes. I accept that it isn't going anywhere any time soon.

"It's better to light a candle than to curse the darkness."
—Eleanor Roosevelt

AUTISM RESOURCES

Autism Speaks
Founded in 2005 by Bob Wright, Vice Chairman of GE and former NBC CEO and his wife, the organization is dedicated to raising awareness of autism spectrum disorders, to funding research, and to advocating for the needs of families affected by the disorder. http://www.autismspeaks.org/

Autism Speaks Transition Tool Kit:
http://www.autismspeaks.org/family-services/tool-kits/transition-tool-kit

The IAN Project
IAN, the Interactive Autism Network, is an online project designed to accelerate the pace of autism research by linking researchers and families. http://www.ianproject.org/

First Signs, Inc.
First Signs is an organization dedicated to the early identification and intervention of children with developmental delays and disorders. http://www.firstsigns.org/

Autism Society of America

One of the main advocacy organizations in the US. The site contains links to many local chapters of ASA. http://www.autism-society.org/

National Institute for Neurological Disorder and Stroke / National Institutes of Health

General autism information site.
http://www.ninds.nih.gov/disorders/autism/detail_autism.htm

Centers For Disease Control (CDC)

Facts about autism, its early signs, diagnosis, and its prevalence.
http://www.cdc.gov/ncbddd/autism/

AWAARE Collaboration

Working to prevent wandering incidents and deaths within the autism community, including an Autism Wandering Emergency Kit:
http://www.awaare.org/

TEACCH (Treatment and Education of Autistic and related Communication-handicapped Children)

An evidence-based service, training, and research program for individuals of all ages and skill levels with autism spectrum disorders.
http://www.teacch.com/

TACA

Talk About Curing Autism (**TACA**) is a national organization dedicated to providing information, resources, and support to families affected by autism. www.tacanow.org

Generation Rescue

Jenny McCarthy's autism organization is dedicated to recovery of children with autism spectrum disorders by providing guidance and support to families. www.generationrescue.org

Epilepsy.com

Epilepsy.com is the #1 online resource and community (blogs, forums, chats) providing in-depth information for people living with **epilepsy** and seizures. www.epilepsy.com

Autism I.D. Cards

Helps people on the autism spectrum explain their medical condition to Police, EMTs, and other first responders in the event of an emergency. http://autismidcard.com/

Autistic Self Advocacy Network

The Autistic Self Advocacy Network is a 501(c)(3) nonprofit organization run by and for autistic people. ASAN's supporters include autistic adults and youth, cross-disability advocates, and non-autistic family members, professionals, educators and friends. ASAN was created to provide support and services to individuals on the autism spectrum while working to educate communities and improve public perceptions of autism. http://autisticadvocacy.org/

The National Suicide Helpline
7 days a week/24 hours per day.
1-800-SUICIDE
1-800-273-TALK
1-800-784-2433
1-800-273-8255

ABOUT THE AUTHOR

Angela Berg Dallara is a wife, mother, autism advocate and writer. With first-hand experience parenting a child with special needs, she tells her story of love and loss with wit and compassion. She is the mother of two boys; her youngest is nonverbal with autism and epilepsy. She lives in Northern California with her family.

Printed in the USA
CPSIA information can be obtained
at www.ICGtesting.com
JSHW022340140824
68134JS00019B/1594

9 781630 470807